TODAY'S

BHAGAVAD GITA

Ancient Wisdom in Modern Rhythm

#International Motivational Trainer

DR. LATESH SHAH

Growth Publication House

Published by **Growth Publication House** [Sujata Mehta, 56 Dev Chhaya, Haji Ali Tardeo Road, Mumbai 400 034 India]

Cover Design by Suraj Vishwakarma
Layout and Design by Suraj Vishwakarma
Book Support: Satesh Khubchandani
Coordination: Hardik Ramtaram Shah

ISBN: 978-81-965256-2-0

First Printing: **August 2025**
Second Edition:
Printed in [MUMBAI]

Distributed by **GROWTH Publication House**, Mumbai, Maharashtra, India.

For **permission requests** or to report any **errors or omissions**, please write to the publisher at the above address or Email Shahlatesh@wh-dc.com

For **bulk purchases, special sales, or corporate sales**, please contact Growth Publishing at **+918779604727/ 9892604506**.

Foreword by Swami Soham Chaitanya Puri

While giving a discourse on The Bhagavad Gita, in Sri Prempuri Adhyatma Vidya Bhavan, Mumbai, I went through a new style of explanation of The Bhagavad Gita by Dr. Latesh Shah.

As we all know, The Bhagavad Gita has, for centuries, shone like a lodestar in the ocean of human consciousness, offering timeless guidance for life's deepest questions. Its teachings, born on a battlefield, remain relevant not just for that era but for every age, every circumstance & every soul. This eternal wisdom has been commented upon again and again by Great Masters for guiding us on the paths of Dharma, Karma, Bhakti, and Jnana. So, the Gita has always been an invitation to unlock the boundless potential hidden within us.

The Gita is not merely a dialogue between a warrior and his charioteer, but a profound conversation between the confused human soul and the divine wisdom within. Lord Krishna's words to Arjuna transcends time, culture, and circumstance — offering clarity in confusion, courage in fear, and purpose amidst chaos.

To the youth, The Gita offers a bold invitation: to live with awareness, to rise in action, and to serve with selflessness. It asks them not to run away from the challenges of life, but to face them with courage and clarity. In its verses lie the seeds of resilience, character, and inner peace — values that are more essential today than ever before.

This prospective modern explanation of The Bhagavad Gita by Dr. Latesh Shah is more than just a book to be read; it is a guide for self-reflection & self-discovery. Dr. Latesh Shah, as a truly spiritual person himself, illuminates the principles of Love, Peace & Wisdom that lie at the very heart of the Gita. They teach us how, by adopting these ancient truths into our daily lives, we can build a more harmonious and purposeful existence.

I trust that readers will find, in this invaluable work, the same inspiration and clarity that I have. "Today's Bhagavad Gita" is not merely a commentary, but an invitation – to awaken the warrior within, to comprehend one's true nature, and to walk the path of compassion & contribution.

With Ashirwad of Bhagawan Kashi Vishwanath,

Swami Soham Chaitanya Puri
Paramarth Sadhak Sangh, Kashi

Foreword by Dr. Bhagyesh Jha

I am delighted to see the book of my dear friend Dr. Latesh Shah on The Bhagavad Gita. I feel thrilled when someone talks about the vital question of '*how to come out from the chaos of modern life'*.

The book is wonderful and its architecture is very attractive, because it talks about human transformation. Let me tell you very briefly that human evolution has come to a very critical juncture where, because of AI, many sciences are merging. Many cultures will also merge. And Bhagavad Gita will be a guiding light in this process of transformation.

The Bhagavad Gita is one great classic masterpiece of wisdom that chronicles the journey of the highly intellectual Arjuna. I was impressed to see Dr. Latesh Shah treating every chapter as a stepping stone on the path towards transformation.

Let us understand that while life is often perceived as an external journey, its truest form is experienced internally, inside the human mind. This inner realm is the key to all future progress and transformation. I am particularly glad that Dr. Shah divided the book in three parts & presented the themes with current context.

As a student of The Bhagavad Gita, I can state with full responsibility, that unless one undergoes through processes and according to the principles enshrined in BG, transformation will not happen with its grand bliss. This process, however, often happens unknowingly. Many people around the world may not know the Bhagavad Gita by name, but they live by its universal message. This book will certainly help bring about a conscious awakening among its readers.

Human history has repeatedly shown that growth is not experienced unless there is an inner transformation. The

Bhagavad Gita has been the handbook of great minds & skilled hands. I am so delighted that Dr. Lateshbhai Shah's "Today's Bhagavad Gita" has addressed the most crucial aspects of this transformative process.

I wish Dr. Latesh Shah the very best & look forward to many more conversations with him on this great handbook for igniting transformation. Let me conclude by saying that we, in India, are blessed as we now have the real Growth Engine, "Today's Bhagavad Gita.

With Warm Regards,

Dr. Bhagyesh Jha (IAS Retd.)
Chairman, Gujarat Sahitya Academy | Sanskrit Scholar & Author
Conjunct Faculty, PDP University
Ph.D. on Bhagavad Gita

Foreword by Deena Mehta

World-famous poet Robert Frost penned the timeless lines:
"Two roads diverged in a wood, and I
I took the one less travelled by,
And that has made all the difference."

Dr. Latesh Shah's life is a shining example of such a choice. From writing 150 one-act dramas and 30 full-length plays, creating films, running successful businesses, and meditating in the Himalayas, to emerging as an international motivational leader—his journey is nothing less than extraordinary. He founded the transformational institute *Growth Vidhyapeeth*, and with decades of experience in touching lives, he now offers a profound modern interpretation of the *Bhagavad Gita*. It is truly amazing.

One of the divine objectives set for every *Gita* reader is to share its message with all those seeking to understand themselves and live joyfully. The *Bhagavad Gita* is not just a scripture—it is a way of life. Through its chapters, it teaches that we need not live in misery, constantly dissatisfied and yearning for more. God is attainable, and all He asks is for us to come closer—through knowledge (*Gyan Yoga*), selfless action (*Karma Yoga*), and love and devotion (*Bhakti Yoga*).

The often-quoted shloka—*"Do not expect the fruits of your labour"*—is, in my view, widely misunderstood. It does not forbid expectations; rather, it reminds us that the results are under God's jurisdiction. If things do not turn out as hoped, trust that what unfolds is in your best interest. This acceptance is what brings lasting peace and bliss.

To summarize the essence of the *Gita* in two words: **discrimination and dedication**. Discriminate between right and wrong, and dedicate every action to God.

In this book, Dr. Latesh Shah has decoded the *Gita* chapter by chapter into a practical, actionable guide for self-realization and happiness. Each chapter is explained in simple, modern English, ending with a to-do list that helps the reader convert learning into daily practice. The *Gita* says we should **live** its message—this book shows you exactly how.

Dr. Latesh Shah has written this book especially for today's youth. This generation faces more competition and change than ever before. In today's fast-paced world, even standing still requires you to run. You face obstacles, pressure, and sometimes failure—yet the *Gita* gently guides you forward. Through its wisdom, God says, *"Keep going, I am with you."* Just as He guided Arjuna, the *Gita* doesn't dictate—it empowers you to make your own decisions with clarity.

In the end, Arjuna says, *"All my doubts are cleared. I will act as per my duty."* That is the ultimate transformation.

I am truly happy to write this foreword, as this book marks an important milestone in spreading the eternal message of the *Gita*. I thank Dr. Latesh Shah for giving me the opportunity to be a part of this divine journey of bringing the *Gita* to the youth.

With Warm Regards,

Deena Mehta
Chartered Accountant | Former President, Stock Exchange
Trustee, Prempuri Ashram
Bhagavad Gita Practitioner

Preface

Finding Solid Ground in a Shifting World

Life today often feels like a **whirlwind**. We're constantly bombarded with information, pulled in countless directions, and pressured to do more, be more, achieve more. **Stress** feels normal, **burnout** is common, and finding **genuine peace** or **lasting purpose** can seem like an impossible task. In this relentless pace, many of us feel **overwhelmed, anxious, and disconnected**, wondering if there's a better way to live.

Where can we find **solid ground** amidst the chaos? Surprisingly, one of the most **potent answers** doesn't come from the latest app or trend, but from **ancient wisdom** whispered thousands of years ago on a battlefield. The **Bhagavad Gita**, often seen as a cornerstone of Hindu philosophy, is far more than a historical or religious text. It's a **profound psychological and spiritual roadmap**, a **timeless guide** to navigating the complexities of life – **your life**, right here, right now.

Think of it as your **secret weapon**, a source of **enduring strength and clarity** specifically designed to help you **thrive**, not just survive, in the demanding modern world.

This book, **"Today's Bhagavad Gita : Ancient Wisdom in Modern Rhythm,"** is designed to be your **practical companion** on this journey of **inner transformation**. We won't just discuss philosophy; we'll actively engage with the Gita's teachings in a way that creates **real change**. You'll find:

- **Deep wisdom clearly explained**
- **Lessons from modern India & timeless icons**
- **Practical exercises for immediate change**

My deepest hope is that this book serves as a **trusted guide**, **empowering** you to step onto your own **inner battlefield**—your personal Kurukshetra—with **courage and wisdom**, transforming chaos into **clarity**, and stress into **unshakable strength**.

"**Today's Bhagavad Gita : Ancient Wisdom in Modern Rhythm**" is a fresh reimagining of India's timeless scripture through the lens of contemporary life. Structured into 18 accessible chapters, the book mirrors the original Gita but with modern relevance—taking readers from emotional paralysis to empowered action.

Dr. Latesh Shah introduces us to Krishna not as a distant deity, but as an inner guide—one who whispers truth in moments of doubt, who urges clarity in the face of conflict. Arjuna's inner battle becomes a metaphor for all of us: struggling with fear, stuck between duty and desire, torn by anxiety and aspiration.

Each chapter unpacks a core human challenge—ego, confusion, over thinking, failure, anger, detachment, purpose—and offers practical tools from the Gita blended with psychological insights and Indian cultural examples. From Swami Vivekananda to Abdul Kalam, from business leaders to saints, the book draws on real-world figures to showcase how Gita's philosophy plays out in action.

What sets this book apart is its actionable design. It includes reflective exercises, storytelling, and relatable language that transforms the Gita from a scriptural monologue into a living dialogue between reader and self.

Ultimately, "**Today's Bhagavad Gita : Ancient Wisdom in Modern Rhythm**" isn't just about understanding ancient verses—it's about awakening the *Krishna* within, calming the *Arjuna* in crisis, and walking boldly into life with clarity, courage, and compassion.

Acknowledgment

Crafting this book has been a journey of profound learning and immense gratitude.

First and foremost, I offer my deepest reverence and gratitude to the timeless wisdom of the Bhagavad Gita and to the divine teacher, Lord Krishna. Its teachings have been a constant source of inspiration and guidance in my own life, and it is a privilege to attempt to share its profound message.

Dedicated to my Brave & Generous Parents

JaverMa & Panchariya Bapa Kariya (Shah)

I am immensely grateful to my family and friends, whose unwavering support and encouragement provided the foundation for this work.

To my teachers and mentors, who have illuminated the path of spiritual understanding, I extend my heartfelt thanks.

I also wish to acknowledge the countless individuals, both historical and contemporary, whose lives exemplify the principles of the Bhagavad Gita. Their real-world experiences, often cited in these pages, bring this ancient wisdom to life and demonstrate its transformative power.

Finally, to You, the reader, for embarking on this journey of self-discovery & transformation. May the wisdom of Gita light your path and bring you peace, purpose & power.

About the Author - Dr. Latesh Shah

Dr Latesh Shah is a versatile personality who has been working successfully in different fields. He is a writer and director who has written 150 one-act plays, 30 full-length plays, three films, and five television serials. His most famous play, Chitkaar, ran for 25 years in Gujarati theatre. He is also a voracious reader, having read thousands of books on various subjects.

With everything he has been doing, the powerful inspiration and goal he has in his life is to transform people with Love, Peace, Knowledge, and Celebration.

He is the Founder-Chairman of Growth Vidhyapeeth, established in 2003. He has been working rigorously through it to transform people's lives, reaching out to over one million people, with the support of coaches he has trained. He has designed and developed courses on a variety of areas like mind, motivation, meditation, money, memory, and business, for transforming people in all areas of their lives. Growth Vidhyapeeth conducts seminars and workshops in many countries like India, Kenya, Mauritius, Thailand, Dubai, UK, USA, South Korea, Hong Kong & more.

Shri Latesh Shah has been honored with the Iconic Honorary Doctorate Award from the Iconic Peace Award Council

(IPAC). This well-deserved recognition celebrates his remarkable impact and dedication to making a difference in society.

His debut book, "I Am Not My Father," was a bestseller. He has also authored other impactful works such as "Fear to Success," "How to Heal Pain," and "How to Be Rich & Wealthy," further cementing his commitment to personal transformation. These literary contributions inspired him to write this book, "“Today's Bhagavad Gita : Ancient Wisdom in Modern Rhythm” This book is yet one more example of fulfilling his intention of reaching out to a broader audience and causing their transformation.

Reading and practicing the principles and action steps of this book will surely bring a positive shift in every reader's life!

Disclaimer

This book, "Today's Bhagavad Gita : Ancient Wisdom in Modern Rhythm" is intended for general informational, educational, and inspirational purposes only. It is based on interpretations of ancient texts and philosophical concepts and aims to provide practical insights for personal growth and well-being in a modern context.

The examples shared in this book are based on actual occurrences from various sources, and specific details may have been altered to maintain the privacy and confidentiality of the individuals involved.

'Errors & Omissions Excepted' (E&OE)

The author acknowledges that every individual's journey is unique, and the experiences shared here are not intended to represent specific outcomes for all readers. It is essential to approach the advice and strategies in this book with an open mind and consider their relevance within your own context. The author does not guarantee any specific results, and the success of implementing the principles discussed in this book may vary from person to person.

Readers are encouraged to exercise their own judgment and discretion while applying the knowledge gained from this book. The author and publisher shall not be held liable for any direct or indirect consequences resulting from the use of the information provided herein.

This book serves as a guide to inspire personal growth and development. Please consult with qualified professionals or seek personalized advice for specific situations that require professional expertise.

Thank you for choosing to embark on this journey of self-discovery and growth with us.

Table of Contents

Introduction

Overwhelmed by Modern Chaos? This Ancient Wisdom is Your Answer

Life today often feels like a whirlwind. We're bombarded with information, pulled in countless directions, and pressured to constantly do more, be more, achieve more. Stress feels normal, burnout is common, and finding genuine peace or lasting purpose can seem like an impossible task. In this relentless pace, many of us feel overwhelmed, anxious, and disconnected, wondering if there's a better way to live. Where can we find solid ground amidst the chaos?

Ancient Wisdom: Your Secret Weapon in Today's World

Surprisingly, one of the most potent answers doesn't come from the latest app or trend, but from ancient wisdom whispered thousands of years ago on a battlefield. The Bhagavad Gita, often seen as a cornerstone of Hindu philosophy, is far more than a historical or religious text. It's a profound psychological and spiritual roadmap, a timeless guide to navigating the complexities of life – your life, right here, right now. Think of it as your secret weapon, a source of enduring strength and clarity specifically designed to help you thrive, not just survive, in the demanding modern world.

Your Inner Battles: Recognizing the Kurukshetra Within

The Gita unfolds on the battlefield of Kurukshetra, where the warrior Arjuna faces an impossible dilemma. But this battlefield isn't just a place in ancient India; it's a powerful metaphor for the inner conflicts we all experience. Your personal Kurukshetra might be navigating difficult relationships, facing career uncertainty, managing stress and anxiety, finding your ethical compass, or simply seeking meaning in your daily existence. The Gita recognizes these inner struggles and offers practical strategies to face them with courage and wisdom.

Your Step-by-Step Transformation: How This Book Guides You

This book is designed to be your practical companion on this journey of inner transformation. We won't just discuss philosophy; we'll actively engage with the Gita's teachings in a way that creates real change. Here's how:

- **Gita Made Simple: Deep Wisdom, Clearly Explained** We'll break down the Gita's profound concepts into straightforward language, making its deep wisdom accessible and easy to grasp, regardless of your prior knowledge.

- **Real People, Real Change: Lessons from Modern India & Timeless Icons** You'll see how these principles apply in the real world through relatable examples, stories, and case studies drawn from modern life alongside timeless figures who embodied this wisdom.

- **Your Transformation Toolkit: Practical Exercises for Immediate Change** Each chapter includes specific, actionable exercises – reflections, meditations, journaling, and practical techniques –

designed to help you integrate the Gita's wisdom into your daily habits and mindset.

Ready for Clarity? Your Journey Begins Now

This book is an invitation to step onto your own inner battlefield, not with fear, but with the Gita as your guide. It's a journey towards understanding yourself more deeply, finding your unique purpose (Dharma), acting with clarity and conviction, and cultivating an unshakeable inner peace that sustains you through life's inevitable ups and downs. If you're ready to move from chaos to clarity, from stress to strength, your journey begins now. Let's explore this transformative wisdom together.

Part I: Face Your Battlefield – Master Your Inner World (Adhyays 1-6)

Welcome to the heart of the battle – not just the epic conflict described in the Mahabharata, but the inner battlefield where your most significant struggles and transformations take place. The first six Adhyays (Chapters) of the Bhagavad Gita delve deep into understanding the nature of this inner conflict, the forces at play within you, and the foundational wisdom needed to navigate your challenges. This part lays the groundwork, helping you recognize your own struggles in Arjuna's dilemma and introducing the core paths – like action, knowledge, and self-control – that lead towards mastery. Facing your battlefield is the first step towards claiming your inner peace and power.

Adhyay 1: Find Strength in Crisis – Turn Rock Bottom into Your Launch pad (Arjuna Vishada Yoga – The Yoga of Arjuna's Despondency)

That Feeling of Being Utterly Stuck

Modern life throws constant demands our way. Juggling careers that consume our time, complex family dynamics, financial pressures, striving for health, and navigating the relentless stream of digital information – it often leaves us feeling breathless, stressed, or deeply disconnected. Perhaps you feel it too, especially living with the vibrant intensity and unique pressures of a city like Mumbai, where ambition often clashes with tradition, and external success doesn't always translate to inner peace. You might be facing an acute crisis – a major setback at work, a painful relationship strain, a daunting ethical dilemma, looming financial worries, or a health concern casting a long shadow. Or maybe it's a more pervasive feeling – a creeping burnout, a lack of clear purpose driving your days, a quiet dissatisfaction despite having achieved what society deems 'successful'. In these moments, you might find yourself procrastinating, withdrawing emotionally, feeling fragile, or simply trapped in loops of anxious thought.

This state of inner turmoil, where clarity dissolves into a fog of anxiety and confusion, where decision-making feels impossible, and the very will to act seems to evaporate – this is *Vishada*. It's a deep despondency, a crisis of spirit that can feel like hitting rock bottom. It's undeniably uncomfortable, yet the Gita presents this state not as a personal failure, but as a potent, often necessary, starting point. It is precisely in these moments of breakdown that the greatest potential for breakthrough often arises. Recognizing and acknowledging this inner state, without layering on judgment, is the first courageous step on the path the Gita unfolds.

Arjuna's Breakdown: A Warrior Overwhelmed

The Bhagavad Gita doesn't begin with abstract philosophy; it plunges us immediately into raw human vulnerability. We meet Arjuna – the epitome of skill, righteousness, and courage – not celebrating his prowess, but at his absolute lowest point. Poised on the Kurukshetra battlefield, ready for a war he intellectually believes is just, he asks his divine guide and charioteer, Krishna, for a clear view of the opposing army.

What Arjuna sees devastates him. It's not just an abstract enemy force; it's a sea of familiar faces reflecting his deepest relational bonds. He sees Bhishma, the patriarch who raised him; Drona, the revered teacher who gifted him his martial skills; beloved cousins, uncles, nephews, friends, teachers – the very fabric of his world, now positioned as adversaries he must potentially kill. For a man whose identity is intrinsically tied to his role as a warrior and protector of Dharma, this sight triggers an existential crisis.

His collapse is visceral and complete:

- **Physical Manifestations:** His limbs weaken ('fail me'), his mouth becomes parched, his body trembles uncontrollably, his hair stands on end ('bristles with horror'), his skin burns, and the mighty Gandiva bow

– the symbol of his strength, duty, and identity – slips uselessly from his grasp.

- **Emotional Flood:** He is completely overcome ('excessively smitten') with pity, profound sorrow, and deep, incapacitating anguish.
- **Mental Paralysis:** His mind reels ('seems to be whirling'), unable to grasp the situation, maintain composure, or see any clear path forward.

Decoding Arjuna's Arguments: Voices of Despair Arjuna's paralysis isn't just a feeling; it fuels specific, powerful arguments against fighting, revealing the depth of his inner conflict:

1. **Compassion & Attachment (Kinship):** His primary cry stems from love and connection. "Seeing my own kinsmen... how can we be happy, O Krishna, killing our own people?" The thought of causing harm to those he loves feels fundamentally wrong, overriding his warrior duty.
2. **Fear of Sin (Papa):** Within his ethical framework, killing relatives, especially respected elders and teachers, constitutes a grave sin. He believes this action will bring immense negative karmic repercussions, leading to suffering in this life and potentially terrible consequences in the hereafter.
3. **Societal Chaos (Kulakṣaya):** His concern extends beyond personal grief. He foresees the destruction of

the family lineage leading to the collapse of vital social structures and traditions (*kuladharma*). This, he fears, will cause widespread impiety (*adharma*) and ultimately lead to the ruin of the entire society.

4. **Profound Confusion about Duty (Dharma):** His entire worldview, built on the Kshatriya (warrior class) code of righteous warfare and upholding social order, crumbles. Faced with this unprecedented horror, he is utterly bewildered about what constitutes right action (*Dharma*) in this situation.

Recognizing his complete inability to resolve this internal conflict, he explicitly turns to Krishna, surrendering his pride and admitting his confusion: "My mind is confused about my duty... I ask you, tell me decisively what is good for me." His final declaration is stark: "I will not fight." He lays down his weapons and slumps onto the chariot seat, overcome by grief. This is not cowardice; it's the profound anguish of a deeply conscientious person facing an ethical and emotional abyss.

Modern Freezes: Recognizing Your Own Kurukshetra

Arjuna's state is a perfect illustration of the human 'freeze' response, well-understood in modern psychology. When faced with a situation perceived as too complex, threatening, or emotionally devastating, our nervous system can effectively shut down our capacity for rational action. We don't fight, we don't flee – we freeze. Arjuna is frozen by the sheer weight of his dilemma.

Where do we encounter this 'freeze' in our modern lives, our own personal Kurukshetras?

Career Paralysis: Feeling trapped in a job you dislike in a competitive city like Delhi or Mumbai, seeing potential paths but terrified of the uncertainty or perceived risk of failure? That inability to act is a freeze.

Relationship Stagnation: Knowing a difficult conversation is essential with a partner, family, or colleague, but avoiding it endlessly due to fear of conflict, hurting feelings, or disrupting the status quo? That avoidance is a form of freeze.

Academic or Creative Blocks: Facing a high-stakes exam or a major creative project and feeling completely unable to start, falling into endless procrastination despite looming deadlines? This freeze often stems from underlying perfectionism or fear of inadequacy.

Ethical Indecision: Witnessing something unjust at work or in your community but feeling unable to speak up or intervene due to fear of repercussions, social awkwardness, or uncertainty about how to act? That silence can be a debilitating freeze.

During such moments, our brain's emotional centers can hijack our prefrontal cortex – the seat of logic, planning, and impulse control. We might experience cognitive overload (too many factors to weigh) or decision fatigue (mental exhaustion from constant choices). Like Arjuna, we might even find ourselves constructing elaborate rationalizations for our inaction, justifications that cleverly mask the underlying fear, confusion, or conflicting desires.

The root cause, the Gita masterfully unfolds throughout its teachings, is often misidentification (*Avidya* – ignorance or delusion). We mistakenly believe our temporary roles, possessions, relationships, or even our thoughts and feelings constitute our true, essential self. We become intensely attached to certain outcomes ("I *must* get this promotion") and develop strong aversions to others ("I *cannot* handle their disapproval"). When a crisis threatens these attachments – our job security, our social image, our comfort zone – it feels like *we* are being threatened at our core. This perceived existential threat triggers the freeze response and immense suffering.

The Wisdom of the Witness: Krishna's Initial Response

Significantly, Krishna doesn't immediately rebuke Arjuna for his despair or jump in with solutions. He simply *listens*. He holds the space, allowing Arjuna to fully express the depths of his anguish, confusion, and conflicting arguments. This, in itself, is the first, crucial, and often overlooked counsel the Gita offers: the profound wisdom of **compassionate witnessing**.

Before genuine transformation can begin, the reality of our inner state – the messy, uncomfortable truth of our fear, confusion, pain, and conflicting desires – must be acknowledged without the immediate overlay of judgment or self-criticism. Our typical inner critic rushes in ("I shouldn't feel this way," "I should be stronger," "I need to just snap out of it!"). Trying to suppress or instantly 'fix' these powerful feelings often backfires, driving them underground or making them stronger. Krishna's initial response teaches us the power of creating inner space. It's about learning to observe the internal storm – the turbulent thoughts, the difficult emotions – without getting swept away, and crucially, without condemning ourselves for having the storm in the first place. Honouring your breakdown, your confusion, your vulnerability as a valid human experience is the essential first step toward any meaningful breakthrough.

Strength Forged in Crisis: Lessons from Inspiring Leaders

Facing deep internal conflict isn't a sign of inadequacy; history and contemporary life show it's often the crucible where true strength, resilience, and clarity of purpose are forged. Consider these brief examples:

Mahatma Gandhi: His unwavering commitment to non-violence required constantly confronting internal battles – weighing the immense risks to himself and his followers against the powerful forces of empire, battling doubt about whether Satyagraha could truly prevail against brute force. His strength emerged from this deep internal alignment achieved through struggle.

JRD Tata: Pioneering industries vital for modern India involved navigating enormous financial risks, complex political landscapes, and internal pressures pushing towards compromise. His legacy rests on consistently choosing the harder, ethical, nation-building path over easier alternatives, a testament to conviction forged amidst challenges.

Rani Lakshmibai: Her legendary defiance against the British annexation of Jhansi wasn't impulsive bravado. It was a conscious choice made against overwhelming odds, requiring her to confront the primal fear for her own life and her people's future, weighing it against her sworn duty (*Dharma*) as a ruler. Her extraordinary courage was born from that impossible conflict.

These figures, among countless others, remind us that facing our own Kurukshetras – our moments of deep doubt, fear, and conflicting values – is not a deviation from the path of strength, but often the path itself.

Chapter 1 Takeaway: Acknowledge Your Battlefield

The essential message, the foundational wisdom of this first Adhyay, lies in the transformative power of honest acknowledgment. Recognizing your moments of crisis, confusion, paralysis, and despair – without layering on shame or judgment – is not weakness. It is, in fact, the crucial first step toward accessing the deeper wisdom and strength that reside within you. By clearly understanding the landscape of your inner battlefield – the conflicting forces, the fears, the attachments – you create the necessary space for clarity to dawn and for the practical solutions offered in the following chapters to take root. Arjuna's raw vulnerability, his willingness to admit "I am stuck," becomes the fertile ground for the entire profound teaching of the Bhagavad Gita.

कर्पण्यदोषोपहतस्वभावः पृच्छामि त्वां धर्मसम्मूढचेताः ।
यच्छ्रेयः स्यान्निश्चितं ब्रूहि तन्मे शिष्यस्तेऽहं शाधि मां त्वां
प्रपन्नम् ॥ २.७ ॥

Kārpaṇya-doṣopahata-svabhāvaḥ pṛcchāmi tvāṁ dharma-sammūḍha-cetāḥ | Yac-chreyaḥ syān-niścitaṁ brūhi tan-me śiṣyas-te'haṁ śādhi māṁ tvāṁ prapannam || 2.7 ||

Hindi: "दीनता के दोष से मेरा स्वभाव दब गया है और धर्म के विषय में मेरा चित्त मोहित हो रहा है। मैं आपसे पूछता हूँ कि जो मेरे लिए निश्चित रूप से कल्याणकारी हो, वह मुझे कहें। मैं आपका शिष्य हूँ, आपकी शरण में आए हुए मुझे शिक्षा दें।"

English: "Now I am confused about my duty and have lost all composure because of miserly weakness. In this condition, I am asking you to tell me for certain what is best for me. Now I am Your disciple, and a soul surrendered unto You. Please instruct me." ***(Arjuna's explicit plea for guidance, marking his readiness to learn)***

Exercise: Mapping Your Inner Battlefield

This exercise helps you gain clarity on your own inner conflict, mirroring Arjuna's situation. Dedicate 25-30 minutes of uninterrupted time. Choose your most significant current challenge where you feel stuck or conflicted. Use a journal. Approach this with honesty and self-compassion – the aim is awareness, not immediate problem-solving.

Describe the Situation: What's happening factually? Who are the key people involved? What is the core challenge, decision, or dilemma you face? Be specific and objective. (e.g., "Deciding whether to relocate for a demanding but high-paying job," "Handling a recurring disagreement with a family member about life choices," "Finding the motivation and discipline to pursue a personal health goal").

Identify Core Conflicts: What are the fundamental tensions pulling you in different directions? List 2-3 primary opposing forces. Phrasing them as "X vs. Y" can be helpful (e.g., "Financial Security vs. Personal Passion/Meaning," "Loyalty to Others vs. Personal Integrity/Ethics," "Maintaining Comfort/Status Quo vs. Potential for Growth/Change," "Meeting Expectations vs. Following My Own Path").

Articulate Inner Arguments (The 'Stuck' Narrative): Write down all the reasons, justifications, or fears your mind offers for feeling stuck or avoiding decisive action. Let the voice of doubt, fear, or confusion speak freely without censorship. (e.g., "If I do X, then Y bad things might happen..." "I don't have enough skill/time/energy/support." "It's safer to do nothing for now." "People will disapprove/be disappointed if I..." "I might regret it later." "It feels too difficult/painful/overwhelming.").

Name Dominant Emotions: Go beyond general terms like "stress." List the specific emotions you feel most strongly when you think about this situation. Aim for 3-5 specific feelings. (e.g., Fear (of failure, judgment, loss, the unknown), Anxiety (about the future), Guilt (about potential impact on others), Resentment (towards demands or situation), Helplessness, Frustration, Sadness, Confusion).

Uncover Attachments & Aversions: What specific outcomes are you desperately attached to achieving? What specific outcomes are you strongly averse to (trying hard to avoid)? What identities, relationships, or states of being feel threatened? Be brutally honest. (e.g., "Attachment to being seen as competent/successful," "Attachment to financial security/stability," "Attachment to this person's approval/love," "Aversion to conflict/disapproval," "Aversion to uncertainty/risk," "Attachment to comfort/the known," "Need to feel in control").

Tune Into Your Body's Signals: Where do you feel this conflict physically in your body? Scan yourself and note any recurring tension, aches, or sensations. (e.g., Tightness in shoulders/neck/jaw, shallow breathing, knots in the stomach, headache, racing heart, overall fatigue, restlessness). Acknowledging the physical manifestation is part of understanding the full impact of the inner conflict.

(Remember, the goal of this exercise isn't to solve the problem right now, but to gain profound clarity on the different elements at play on your inner battlefield. This conscious awareness is the essential foundation for effectively applying the wisdom and solutions explored in the following chapters.)

Adhyay 2: Discover the Unshakeable You – Go Beyond Roles to Find Your True Self

(Sankhya Yoga – The Yoga of Analytical Knowledge)

From Despair to Discernment: Krishna Responds

In the previous chapter, we witnessed Arjuna's complete breakdown – paralyzed by grief, confusion, and conflicting duties on the precipice of war. He surrendered his own judgment, acknowledging his profound confusion about Dharma (right action) and pleading with Krishna for clear guidance (as reflected in BG 2.7). Adhyay 2 marks the beginning of Krishna's profound response. He doesn't immediately offer simple solutions or platitudes. Instead, he starts by laying a foundation of transformative knowledge, shifting Arjuna's perspective from the immediate emotional turmoil to the fundamental nature of reality and the self. This is *Sankhya Yoga*, the yoga of analytical knowledge, the path of discerning the real from the unreal, the eternal from the temporary. It's the starting point for understanding *why* Arjuna's grief, though understandable, is ultimately based on a misunderstanding of his true identity and the nature of existence.

Reality Check: Distinguishing Eternal Truth from the Temporary World

Krishna's first strike against Arjuna's despondency is aimed at the impermanent nature of worldly experiences. He points out that sensory perceptions – leading to feelings of happiness and distress, heat and cold, pleasure and pain – are fleeting. They arise from the contact of the senses with their objects, and they inevitably come and go, like the changing seasons. They appear, and they disappear.

Think about your own life. Moments of intense joy fade. Periods of deep sorrow eventually pass. Successes are followed by challenges, and failures by new opportunities. Physical sensations, emotional states, external circumstances – all are in constant flux. Yet, we often invest enormous emotional energy in clinging to pleasant experiences and desperately avoiding unpleasant ones, forgetting their transient nature. This constant chasing and resisting, based on temporary states, becomes a primary source of our suffering and mental agitation.

Krishna advises Arjuna (and us) to learn to tolerate these inevitable dualities without being disturbed. This doesn't mean becoming unfeeling or suppressing emotions. It means developing *Titiksha* – forbearance, endurance, equanimity. It's about cultivating an inner stability that isn't rocked by the inevitable ups and downs of life. By understanding that these experiences are temporary phenomena passing through our awareness, we can stop giving them the power to define our inner state. This realization is the first step toward finding lasting peace amidst the world's constant change.

Meet Your Immortal Self: Understanding the Atman Beyond the Physical Body

Having addressed the temporary nature of external experiences, Krishna unveils the cornerstone of Sankhya philosophy: the distinction between the physical body (*Deha*) and the true Self (*Atman* or *Dehi* - the dweller within the body). This is perhaps the most crucial understanding for overcoming the fear of death and loss that paralyzes Arjuna.

Krishna declares that the *Atman*, the real Self residing within each living being, is:

Eternal (Nitya): It has always existed and will always exist. It has no beginning and no end.

Unborn (Aja): It is not created at the time of physical birth.

Indestructible (Avinashi): It cannot be cut by weapons, burned by fire, moistened by water, or withered by wind. It is impervious to physical destruction.

Unchanging (Avikarya): It does not undergo modifications like birth, growth, decay, and death, which pertain only to the physical body.

All-Pervading (Sarva-gata): It is present everywhere.

In stark contrast, the physical body is temporary. It is born, it grows, it stays for a while, produces by-products, dwindles, and eventually dies. Krishna uses the famous analogy of changing clothes: just as a person discards worn-out garments and puts on new ones, the embodied soul (Atman) similarly discards worn-out bodies and accepts new ones.

This teaching directly addresses Arjuna's grief over the potential death of his relatives and teachers. Krishna points out that the true Self of these individuals cannot be slain. What he fears destroying is merely the temporary physical form, not the eternal essence. Understanding this distinction is revolutionary. It shifts our identity from the fragile, perishable body and the roles associated with it (father, son, teacher, student, professional) to the invulnerable, eternal Self within. This realization is the antidote to the fear of death, loss, and change that underlies so much human suffering. It helps us understand that who we truly are is untouched by the fate of the physical body.

Ancient Wisdom & Modern Psychology: Insights on Ego, Identity, and Your Core Self

The Gita's concept of the Atman versus the body/mind complex resonates deeply with modern psychological explorations of identity, ego, and consciousness. While psychology uses different terminology, the core insights overlap significantly.

Ego and Misidentification: Psychology recognizes the 'ego' as a constructed sense of self, built from our experiences, roles, beliefs, memories, and social conditioning. This ego often mistakenly identifies itself with the body, possessions, achievements, or social status – the very misidentification (*Avidya*) the Gita highlights. Much psychological suffering arises from threats to this constructed ego-identity. When we face failure, rejection, loss, or aging, the ego feels attacked, leading to anxiety, depression, and defensive behaviours.

The Search for the Core Self: Many psychological and contemplative traditions encourage looking beyond the fluctuating ego to find a more stable, authentic 'core self' or 'observing self'. This aligns with the Gita's concept of the Atman as the unchanging witness behind the activities of the mind and body. Practices like mindfulness, common in both therapy & meditation, help cultivate this awareness, allowing us to see thoughts, feelings, and sensations as temporary events rather than defining who we are.

Transcending Ego-Based Suffering: Both the Gita and certain psychologies suggest that liberation from suffering involves loosening the grip of the ego and realizing our connection to something deeper and more enduring. By understanding that "I am not just my thoughts," "I am not just my job," "I am not just this temporary body," we gain psychological flexibility and resilience. We suffer less from life's inevitable changes because our core sense of self is anchored in the unchanging Atman, not the fleeting ego-constructs.

Sankhya Yoga, therefore, isn't just ancient philosophy; it's a profound psychological insight into the nature of identity. It provides a framework for understanding why we suffer due to attachment and misidentification, and it points towards the realization of our true, eternal Self as the path to lasting inner freedom and peace.

Chapter 2 Takeaway: Knowledge That Liberates

The foundational knowledge presented in this chapter – understanding the temporary nature of the world and the eternal nature of the true Self (Atman) – is the bedrock upon which the rest of the Gita's teachings stand. This wisdom directly addresses the root of Arjuna's fear and grief. By discerning the real from the unreal, the permanent from the impermanent, we begin to untangle ourselves from the suffering caused by attachment and misidentification. This analytical knowledge (*Sankhya*) provides the crucial perspective needed to face life's challenges with courage, & clarity, paving the way for understanding right action (*Karma Yoga*), which Krishna will elaborate on next.

न जायते म्रियते वा कदाचिन् नायं भूत्वा भविता वा न भूयः। अजो नित्यः शाश्वतोऽयं पुराणो न हन्यते हन्यमाने शरीरे ॥ २.२० ॥

Na jāyate mriyate vā kadāchin nāyaṁ bhūtvā bhavitā vā na bhūyaḥ | Ajo nityaḥ śāśvato 'yaṁ purāṇo na hanyate hanyamāne śarīre || 2.20 ||

Hindi: "यह आत्मा किसी काल में भी न तो जन्मता है और न मरता ही है तथा न यह उत्पन्न होकर फिर होनेवाला ही है। क्योंकि यह अजन्मा, नित्य, सनातन और पुरातन है। शरीर के मारे जाने पर भी यह नहीं मारा जाता।"

English: "For the soul (Atman) there is neither birth nor death at any time. He has not come into being, does not come into being, and will not come into being. He is unborn, eternal, ever-existing and primeval. He is not slain when the body is slain." ***(A key verse describing the eternal nature of the true Self)***

Exercise: Cultivating the Observer – Disidentifying from the Temporary

This exercise helps you practice distinguishing your true Self (the observer) from the temporary phenomena of body, thoughts, and emotions, fostering objectivity and clarity. Dedicate 10-15 minutes in a quiet space.

1. **Find a Comfortable Posture:** Sit comfortably, either on a chair with your feet flat on the floor or cross-legged on a cushion. Gently close your eyes.

2. **Tune into Body Sensations:** Bring your awareness to the physical sensations in your body. Notice areas of contact (feet on floor, body on chair/cushion). Notice any tension, warmth, coolness, tingling, or pulsing. Simply observe these sensations without judging them or trying to change them. Acknowledge: "There are sensations happening in the body. I am aware of observing these sensations." Repeat this acknowledgment silently a few times.

3. **Observe the Breath:** Gently bring your attention to your breath. Notice the natural rhythm of inhalation and exhalation. Feel the air moving in and out. Don't control the breath; just observe it as it is. Acknowledge: "Breathing is happening. I am aware of observing the breath."

4. **Watch Thoughts Come and Go:** Become aware of thoughts arising in your mind. Notice them like clouds passing in the sky. Don't engage with them, analyze them, or judge them (whether pleasant or unpleasant). Simply note their presence and watch them drift by. Acknowledge: "Thoughts are arising

and passing. I am aware of observing these thoughts." If you get caught up in a thought, gently guide your attention back to observing.

5. **Notice Emotions:** Become aware of any emotions present right now (calmness, boredom, anxiety, peace, etc.). Observe the feeling tone without getting lost in the story behind the emotion. Where do you feel it in your body? Acknowledge: "Emotions are present. I am aware of observing these emotions."

6. **Rest in Awareness:** For the final few minutes, simply rest in the state of being the observer – the silent, still awareness behind all the changing phenomena (sensations, breath, thoughts, emotions). Recognize this awareness as your underlying stable presence.

(Practice this regularly, even for short periods. It gradually strengthens your ability to disidentify from temporary states and cultivate the calm objectivity that comes from recognizing your true nature as the unchanging observer, the Atman.)

Adhyay 3: Act with Purpose, Not Stress – Unlock Power in Your Daily Duties

(Karma Yoga – The Yoga of Action)

The Dilemma of Action: If Knowledge is Key, Why Act?

In Adhyay 2, Krishna unveiled profound wisdom (*Sankhya Yoga*), emphasizing the eternal nature of the true Self (Atman) and the fleeting, impermanent quality of the material world and its experiences. He highlighted that the wise remain undisturbed by pleasure and pain, understanding the indestructible reality of the Self beyond the perishable body. This powerful knowledge aimed to dispel Arjuna's grief and fear.

However, this very emphasis on knowledge and detachment can lead to a natural question, which Arjuna himself implicitly raises: If knowledge and understanding the eternal Self are superior, why then engage in a violent, gruesome action like warfare? Why not renounce all action and simply focus on acquiring wisdom? This sets the stage for Krishna to explain *Karma Yoga*, the yoga of selfless action, revealing that action itself, when performed with the right understanding and attitude, is not only unavoidable but also a powerful path to liberation and inner peace.

Selfless Action Explained: Performing Duty (Dharma) Without Attachment to Results

Krishna begins by clarifying that no one can remain inactive even for a moment. The very forces of material nature (*Prakriti*) compel everyone to act. Simply trying to abstain from action physically, while the mind still dwells on sense objects or desires, is hypocrisy and achieves nothing. Even the basic maintenance of our physical body requires constant action. Therefore, the question isn't *whether* to act, but *how* to act in a way that doesn't create further bondage and stress.

This is where Karma Yoga comes in. It's the art & science of:

1. **Performing Your Prescribed Duty (Dharma):** Everyone has their *Svadharma* – inherent duties or responsibilities based on their nature (*Svabhava*), societal role, and stage of life. These aren't just professional tasks but encompass our responsibilities towards family, society, and our own well-being. Krishna emphasizes that performing one's own Dharma, even if imperfectly, is far better than trying to perform another's duty, however perfectly. Engaging in your natural duties diligently is essential for maintaining individual and cosmic order.

2. **Working Without Attachment (Asanga):** This is the cornerstone of Karma Yoga. It means performing your actions with full dedication, skill, and enthusiasm, but renouncing attachment to the *fruits* or results of those actions. Success or failure, gain or loss, praise or blame – these are external outcomes that are often not entirely within our control. Attachment to these outcomes creates anxiety before

the action, agitation during the action, and either elation (leading to ego) or despair (leading to suffering) after the action.

3. **Action Without Selfish Desire (Nishkama Karma):** Actions should be performed not for the gratification of personal, selfish desires, but for a higher purpose or as one's duty. When actions are driven by ego and selfish cravings, they bind us to the cycle of karma and its repercussions.

4. **Working for the Sake of Yajna (Sacrifice):** Krishna introduces the concept of *Yajna*, often translated as sacrifice. In a broader sense, any action performed with a selfless spirit, for the welfare of others, for the maintenance of cosmic order, or as an offering to a higher principle (be it God, humanity, or a noble ideal) can be considered Yajna. When work is done in this spirit of offering, it purifies the mind and doesn't create karmic bondage.

By performing actions with this attitude of detachment, dedication to duty, and a spirit of selfless offering, work itself is transformed. Instead of being a source of stress, anxiety, and entanglement, it becomes a means of spiritual purification, leading to inner peace, clarity, and ultimately, liberation (*Moksha*).

Historical Grit: Indian Examples of Persistence and Resilience in Action

Indian history, rich and diverse, offers numerous examples of individuals who embodied the principles of Karma Yoga, showcasing exceptional dedication to their duty and purpose without being solely driven by personal gain or deterred by immense challenges.

Sardar Vallabhbhai Patel: After India's independence in 1947, the monumental task of integrating over 500 princely states into the Indian Union fell largely on Sardar Patel. This required immense political skill, unwavering determination, and the ability to act decisively amidst complex and often volatile situations. He performed his duty with a singular focus on unifying the nation, often facing significant opposition, but driven by a larger purpose rather than personal ambition. His actions demonstrate a profound commitment to *Dharma* for national well-being.

Savitribai Phule & Jyotirao Phule: This pioneering couple dedicated their lives to education and social reform in 19th-century India, particularly for women and lower-caste individuals who were denied these opportunities. They faced severe social ostracism, harassment, and lack of resources. Yet, they persisted in their mission to establish schools and fight against discriminatory practices, driven by a deep sense of social justice and the welfare of others. Their relentless action, in the face of extreme adversity, exemplifies performing one's duty selflessly for a transformative cause.

Dr. A.P.J. Abdul Kalam: From humble beginnings to becoming the President of India and a revered scientist, Dr. Kalam's life was a testament to dedicated action and lifelong learning. His work in India's missile development program and his later role as a statesman were marked by immense dedication to his responsibilities and a desire to inspire the youth of India. He often spoke about working with passion and purpose, emphasizing contribution over personal reward, reflecting key tenets of Karma Yoga.

These figures, though operating in different spheres, illustrate the power of focused, dedicated action performed with a sense of duty and resilience, often with benefits extending far beyond their own lives.

Conquer Fear Through Action: Strategies to Overcome Hesitation and Doubt

Arjuna's paralysis stemmed from fear – fear of loss, fear of sin, fear of societal chaos. Karma Yoga provides a powerful antidote to such fear and the hesitation it breeds. When we are overly attached to the results of our actions, fear becomes our constant companion: fear of not achieving the desired outcome, fear of judgment, fear of failure. This fear can lead to procrastination, avoidance, or half-hearted efforts.

Krishna's counsel to act according to one's Dharma, without attachment to the fruits, directly addresses this:

Focus on the Action, Not the Outcome: By shifting your primary focus from "What will I get?" or "What if I fail?" to "How can I perform this action to the best of my ability, as my duty?" you liberate a tremendous amount of mental energy. Your concentration improves, and the action itself becomes more skillful.

Action as an Offering: When you dedicate your work to a higher purpose – be it your family's well-being, service to the community, the pursuit of knowledge, or a spiritual ideal – the personal stakes diminish. The action becomes less about *your* success or failure and more about your contribution. This lessens the ego's involvement and the fear associated with it.

Embrace Your Duty (Dharma): Knowing that you are performing your prescribed duty, what is naturally yours to do, provides a sense of rightness and stability. This intrinsic motivation can override the fear of external criticism or temporary setbacks.

Detachment Neutralizes Fear of Loss: If you are not attached to a specific outcome (e.g., a promotion, public acclaim, a particular financial gain), then the possibility of not achieving it no longer holds the same terror. You can act boldly and with integrity, knowing you did your best, regardless of the result.

Action Dispels Inertia: Sometimes, the best way to overcome fear is simply to begin acting. Inertia and fear often feed each other. Taking the first small step, even if imperfectly, can build momentum and reduce the perceived enormity of the task and the associated anxiety.

By cultivating these attitudes, the Karma Yogi learns to act with courage and conviction, transforming fear from a paralyzing force into a manageable emotion that no longer dictates their choices or inhibits their duty.

Chapter 3 Takeaway: Work as Worship, Action as Freedom

Karma Yoga revolutionizes our understanding of work and action. It teaches that any action, from the mundane to the monumental, can become a path to spiritual growth and inner peace if performed with the right attitude: dedication to duty, skillfulness, detachment from results, and a spirit of selfless offering. It shifts the focus from the *outcome* of action to the *quality and intention* of the action itself. This path liberates us from the stress, anxiety, and bondage typically associated with work driven by selfish desires and attachment, allowing us to engage with the world purposefully and joyfully. Action, performed as Karma Yoga, ceases to be a burden and becomes a form of worship, a means to connect with our true Self and contribute to the world without losing our inner equilibrium.

कर्मण्येवाधिकारस्ते मा फलेषु कदाचन । मा कर्मफलहेतुर्भूर्मा ते सङ्गोऽस्त्वकर्मणि ॥ ३.४७ ॥ (This verse is actually BG 2.47, but it's the quintessential Karma Yoga verse and often discussed in the context of Adhyay 3's themes. A direct verse from Adhyay 3 could be 3.19 or 3.30. Let's use 3.19 for thematic consistency with Adhyay 3 if preferred, or stick with 2.47 for its ubiquity. Given the context of selfless action being paramount in Adhyay 3, let's use 3.19 for now.)

तस्मादसक्तः सततं कार्यं कर्म समाचर । असक्तो ह्याचरन्कर्म परमाप्नोति पूरुषः ॥ ३.१९ ॥

Tasmād-asaktaḥ satataṁ kāryaṁ karma samāchara | Asakto hy-ācharan-karma param-āpnoti pūruṣaḥ || 3.19 ||

Hindi: "इसलिए तुम अनासक्त होकर सदा कर्तव्य कर्म करो। क्योंकि अनासक्त होकर कर्म करने से मनुष्य परमात्मा को प्राप्त होता है।"

English: "Therefore, without being attached to the fruits of activities, one should act as a matter of duty, for by working without attachment one attains the Supreme." ***(This verse emphasizes performing duty without attachment to attain the highest.)***

Exercise: Mindful Action – Performing Duty with Detachment

This exercise helps you practice the principles of Karma Yoga in your daily life, focusing on performing an action with dedication while cultivating detachment from the specific outcome.

Identify a 'Duty' or Task: Choose a specific task or duty you need to perform today or this week. It could be a work assignment, a household chore, a commitment to someone, or even a personal development activity. It should be an action you tend to feel some attachment to the outcome of, or perhaps some resistance or stress towards.

Set Your Intention (The 'Why'): Before you begin, take a moment to clarify your intention. Why are you doing this?

- Can you connect it to your broader sense of duty (Dharma) – professional, familial, societal?
- Can you frame it as an offering or service, even in a small way (e.g., cleaning for the well-being of your home, completing a report for the smooth functioning of your team)?
- Consciously decide to focus on performing the action well, rather than solely on the expected reward, recognition, or specific result.

Engage with Full Attention (The 'How'):

- As you perform the task, bring your full attention to the process itself. Engage your senses. Notice the details of what you are doing.
- If your mind wanders to future outcomes (e.g., "Will they like this?" "What if it doesn't work out?" "I hope I get praised for this."), gently acknowledge the thought and bring your focus back to the present action.
- Perform the action with care, diligence, and to the best of your current ability, without excessive anxiety about perfection or fear of imperfection.

Practice Letting Go of the Outcome:

As you work, and especially upon completion, consciously practice releasing your attachment to the specific result. Remind yourself: "My duty is to perform the action to the best of my ability. The outcome is not entirely in my control, and I accept whatever it may be."

Notice any feelings of anxiety, hope, or fear related to the outcome. Acknowledge these feelings without judgment, and then gently let them go, reaffirming your focus on having done your part.

Reflect Briefly: After completing the action, take a few moments to reflect:

- How did it feel to perform the action with this shift in intention and focus?
- Was there less stress or anxiety compared to usual?
- Did you feel a greater sense of peace or satisfaction from the act of doing, rather than just the potential outcome?
- What was challenging about practicing detachment?

(This is a practice. Don't expect perfection. With consistent effort, you can gradually cultivate the ability to act with purpose and dedication while remaining free from the stress of attachment to results, transforming your daily work into a path of inner growth.)

Adhyay 4: Ignite Your Inner Wisdom – Turn Knowledge into Life-Changing Insight

(Jnana Karma Sanyasa Yoga – The Yoga of Knowledge, Disciplined Action, and Renunciation)

Knowledge That Liberates: Beyond Action Alone

In Adhyay 3, Krishna masterfully explained *Karma Yoga*, the path of selfless action, revealing how performing our duties without attachment to their fruits can purify the mind and lead to inner peace, rather than further bondage. We learned that action is inevitable and essential. However, one might wonder: Is dedicated action, even when selfless, enough on its own? Or is there a deeper understanding required to navigate the complexities of life and action truly effectively?

Arjuna's journey, and ours, now moves towards understanding the profound role of spiritual knowledge (*Jnana*) in illuminating the path of action and, ultimately, in achieving liberation. Krishna introduces *Jnana Karma Sanyasa Yoga* by revealing the ancient lineage of this sacred wisdom, emphasizing that this knowledge, when truly understood and integrated, has the power to burn away the effects of past actions and reveal our true nature. It's about understanding not just *how* to act, but *what* action truly is, *who* the real actor is, and what the ultimate purpose of all our endeavors might be. This chapter focuses on how divine knowledge ignites a transformative inner wisdom.

The Path of Self-Inquiry: Using Knowledge for Inner Growth

Jnana Yoga is the path of spiritual wisdom, the disciplined pursuit of understanding the fundamental truths of existence. It is not merely an intellectual accumulation of information from scriptures or philosophies, but a profound, experiential realization that dispels the root cause of suffering: ignorance (*Avidya*). This ignorance is primarily the misidentification of our true Self (Atman) with the temporary body, mind, ego, and the fleeting experiences of the material world.

The core of Jnana Yoga involves:

1. **Discernment (Viveka):** Cultivating the ability to distinguish between the real and the unreal, the eternal and the temporary, the Self and the non-Self. This analytical understanding helps us see through the illusions that bind us.

2. **Self-Inquiry (Atma Vichara):** This is the introspective practice of investigating the nature of our own consciousness. It often begins with fundamental questions like, "Who am I?" beyond all the labels, roles, and conditionings we've acquired. It's an inward journey to discover the silent, unchanging witness behind all our thoughts, emotions, and experiences.

3. **Understanding the Nature of Reality:** Jnana Yoga seeks to comprehend the nature of the individual soul (Atman), the Supreme (Brahman or Paramatma), the material world (Prakriti or Maya), and the intricate relationship between them. It explores how the interplay of the three Gunas (fundamental qualities of nature – Sattva, Rajas, Tamas, which will be detailed later) influences our thoughts, actions, and perceptions.

4. **The Role of Guidance:** Traditionally, this path emphasizes the importance of learning from a self-realized Guru (spiritual teacher) and studying sacred scriptures (like the Upanishads and the Bhagavad Gita itself). A qualified guide can help navigate the subtleties of this knowledge and prevent misinterpretation. However, personal reflection, contemplation, and a sincere quest for truth are equally indispensable.

This pursuit of knowledge isn't meant to lead to inaction. Instead, true wisdom illuminates the right way to act. It reveals that while actions themselves are performed by the modes of material nature, the true Self is the detached observer. This understanding allows one to engage in the world effectively without becoming entangled in the karmic consequences of actions, performing them as an offering or as a divine play.

The Science of Self-Awareness: Neuroscientific & Cognitive Perspectives

While Jnana Yoga is an ancient spiritual path, its core principles and practices find intriguing parallels and support in modern neuroscience and cognitive psychology. The quest to understand the self, consciousness, and the workings of the mind is a shared human endeavor.

- **Neuroplasticity and Mind Training:** Practices central to Jnana Yoga, such as meditation, focused contemplation, and self-inquiry, involve training the mind. Neuroscience has demonstrated the principle of neuroplasticity – the brain's ability to reorganize itself by forming new neural connections throughout life. Sustained mental training through these practices can demonstrably alter brain structure and function, leading to increased self-awareness, emotional regulation, and attentional control.

- **Metacognition (Thinking About Thinking):** Jnana Yoga heavily emphasizes observing one's own thought processes without necessarily identifying with them. This is closely related to the psychological concept of metacognition. Developing metacognitive skills allows individuals to become more aware of their cognitive biases, habitual thought patterns, and emotional reactions, which is a crucial step in transforming them.

- **Mindfulness and the Default Mode Network:** The Gita's call to witness the mind resonates with mindfulness practices, which are now widely recognized for their psychological benefits. Research suggests that mindfulness can reduce activity in the brain's "default mode network" (DMN), which is associated with mind-wandering, rumination, and self-referential thought – often sources of anxiety and unhappiness. A quieter DMN can lead to greater presence and clarity.

- **The Constructed Self (Ego):** Modern psychology, particularly fields like narrative psychology and social constructionism, explores how our sense of self (ego) is largely a story we construct based on our experiences, memories, and social interactions. This aligns with Jnana Yoga's assertion that the limited ego is not our ultimate identity and that true freedom comes from realizing a deeper, more fundamental Self (Atman) beyond this constructed identity.

These parallels suggest that the ancient insights into the mind and self, arrived at through deep introspection, are now being complemented by scientific investigation, affirming the timeless relevance of self-awareness practices for human well-being.

Real-World Application: Using Self-Knowledge for Personal & Professional Growth

The pursuit of self-knowledge as described in Jnana Yoga is not an esoteric escape from life but a profound means to engage with it more effectively, peacefully, and purposefully. Its practical applications are vast:

Personal Growth:

- **Emotional Resilience:** By understanding your true Self as distinct from fleeting emotions and external events, you develop greater stability. You're less likely to be overwhelmed by temporary setbacks or aversions.

- **Reduced Stress and Anxiety:** Disidentifying from the ego's constant worries, fears, and desires brings immense relief. You learn to observe anxious thoughts without becoming consumed by them.

- **Improved Relationships:** With less ego-driven defensiveness and a clearer understanding of your own and others' deeper nature, relationships can become more compassionate, authentic, and less prone to conflict.

- **Clarity in Decision-Making:** Self-knowledge helps you connect with your core values, leading to decisions that are more aligned with your true purpose, rather than being driven by fleeting impulses or external pressures.

- **Greater Inner Peace:** Ultimately, understanding your unchanging, eternal nature as the Atman fosters a deep sense of contentment and peace that is independent of external circumstances.

Professional Growth:

- **Enhanced Focus and Concentration:** A mind trained through self-awareness and meditation is less distracted, leading to improved productivity and efficiency.

- **Wise Leadership:** Leaders who possess self-knowledge are often more empathetic, ethical, and capable of making decisions for the greater good, without being swayed by personal ego or short-term gains. They inspire trust and act with greater wisdom.
- **Ethical Conduct:** A deeper understanding of interconnectedness and the true Self naturally fosters ethical behavior and integrity.
- **Increased Creativity:** A quieter, more observant mind is often more open to new ideas and innovative solutions.
- **Stress Management:** Self-knowledge provides powerful tools to navigate workplace pressures, conflicts, and uncertainties with greater equanimity and resilience, reducing the risk of burnout.

By understanding who you truly are beyond your professional title or personal circumstances, you unlock a source of inner strength and wisdom that enriches every aspect of your life.

Chapter 4 Takeaway: Wisdom that Burns Karma and Ignites Freedom

Jnana Yoga, the path of knowledge, is presented by Krishna as a sacred fire that, when kindled through sincere inquiry and practice, has the power to burn all the karmic residues of past actions to ashes. This profound spiritual wisdom doesn't just inform; it transforms. It dispels the darkness of ignorance (*Avidya*), revealing our true, eternal nature as the Atman. This realization is the ultimate freedom – freedom from the illusion of separateness, freedom from the chains of attachment and aversion, and freedom from the cycle of suffering. When complemented by selfless action (Karma Yoga), this divine knowledge empowers us to live a life of purpose, peace, and unshakable clarity, fully engaged with the world yet untouched by its dualities.

यथैधांसि समिद्धोऽग्निर्भस्मसात्कुरुतेऽर्जुन ।
ज्ञानाग्निः सर्वकर्माणि भस्मसात्कुरुते तथा ॥४.३७ ॥
(Excerpt from the second half of BG 4.37)

Yathaidhāṁsi samiddho 'gnir bhasmasāt kurute' arjuna |

Jñānāgniḥ sarva-karmāṇi bhasmasāt kurute tathā || 4.37 ||
(Full verse for context, though only the latter part is usually quoted for the "fire of knowledge" analogy)

Hindi: "हे अर्जुन! जैसे प्रज्वलित अग्नि ईंधनों को भस्ममय कर देती है, वैसे ही ज्ञानरूप अग्नि सम्पूर्ण कर्मों को भस्ममय कर देती है।"

English: "O Arjuna, as the blazing fire turns firewood to ashes, so does the fire of knowledge burn to ashes all reactions to material activities." ***(This verse powerfully***

illustrates the purifying and liberating nature of true spiritual knowledge.)

Exercise: Igniting Clarity Through Meditation & Journaling

This section offers two practices to help you cultivate self-awareness and clarity, aligning with the Jnana Yoga.

1. Meditation for Self-Inquiry (10-15 minutes):

- **Settle In:** Find a quiet place where you won't be disturbed. Sit comfortably with your spine relatively straight but not stiff. Gently close your eyes. Take a few deeper breaths to relax your body and mind.

- **Observe Your Thoughts:** Allow your thoughts to come and go without trying to control or suppress them. Simply observe them as if they were clouds passing in the sky. Don't get attached to any particular thought; just notice its presence and let it drift by.

- **Introduce Gentle Inquiry:** After a few minutes of observation, silently and gently pose one of the following questions to yourself:

    - "Who is aware of these thoughts?"

    - "To whom do these thoughts appear?"

    - "Who am I, beyond these thoughts and feelings?"

- **Rest in Awareness:** Don't strain for an answer or expect a dramatic revelation. The purpose is not to find an intellectual answer but to shift your identification from the thoughts themselves to the awareness that perceives them. Rest in this silent, observing awareness. If your mind becomes very active, gently return to observing the breath for a minute, then reintroduce the inquiry.

- **Conclude:** After your allotted time, gently bring your awareness back to your body and your surroundings. Open your eyes slowly.

2. Journaling for Self-Reflection & Clarity:

Set aside 15-20 minutes with a journal. Choose one or more of the following themes to explore:

- **Unpacking a Reaction:** "Think about a recent situation where you had a strong emotional reaction (e.g., anger, sadness, anxiety, extreme joy). Describe the situation briefly. Then, explore: What specific thoughts were going through your mind? What beliefs or assumptions about yourself, others, or the situation might have fueled this reaction? What role or identity felt threatened or validated at that moment?"

- **Examining Limiting Beliefs:** "What are some recurring limiting beliefs you hold about yourself (e.g., 'I'm not good enough,' 'I always fail at X,' 'I need everyone's approval')? Where might these beliefs have originated? How do these beliefs impact your daily actions, decisions, and feelings? What might be a more empowering, truthful perspective?"

- **Identifying Attachments and Aversions:** "Make a list of things, outcomes, or states you feel strongly attached to (e.g., success in your career, financial security, specific relationships, being liked). Then, list things you have a strong aversion to (e.g., failure, criticism, loneliness, uncertainty). How do these attachments and aversions influence your peace of mind and your choices?"

- **Connecting with Your 'Observer Self':** "Reflect on a moment when you were able to observe your thoughts or emotions without getting carried away by them. What did that feel like? What helped you maintain that observer's perspective? How could you cultivate this state more often in your daily life?"

(Engage with these practices regularly. Self-inquiry meditation helps you experientially touch the awareness beyond thought, while reflective journaling brings unconscious patterns and beliefs into conscious awareness, both paving the way for deeper clarity and insight.)

Adhyay 5: Live Free While Engaged – Detach from Drama, Not from Life

(Karma Sanyasa Yoga – The Yoga of Renunciation in Action)

The Path of Wise Action: Renunciation or Engagement?

In Adhyay 3, Krishna emphasized the necessity of action (*Karma Yoga*), performed selflessly and as a matter of duty. In Adhyay 4, he glorified spiritual knowledge (*Jnana Yoga*), revealing it as the fire that purifies all actions and leads to liberation. This naturally brings Arjuna (and us) to a crucial point of inquiry: Which path is superior? Is it better to renounce actions altogether and dedicate oneself solely to the pursuit of knowledge (*Sanyasa*)? Or is it better to remain engaged in the world, performing actions selflessly (*Karma Yoga*)?

Krishna's answer in this chapter resolves this apparent dichotomy. He explains that both paths, if followed sincerely, lead to the ultimate goal. However, he clarifies that true renunciation is not merely the external abandonment of actions, which can be difficult and even hypocritical if the mind remains attached and agitated. True *Sanyasa* is an inner state – the renunciation of selfish desires, attachment to the fruits of action, and the egoistic sense of "I am the doer." He reveals that *Karma Yoga*, the path of selfless action performed with detachment, is often more practical and easier for most people to follow, and it effectively leads to the same state of inner freedom as true renunciation. This chapter, therefore, focuses on *Karma*

Sanyasa Yoga – how to live a life of dynamic action while cultivating the inner freedom of a true renunciate.

Balanced Living: Harmonizing Duty with Inner Renunciation of Ego

The Gita redefines *Sanyasa* (renunciation) not as running away from the world, but as mastering our inner relationship with it. True renunciation isn't about giving up your responsibilities, family, or work; it's about giving up the internal clutches of:

1. **Attachment to Results:** The constant craving for specific outcomes (success, praise, profit) and the Rue deity that accompanies this craving.
2. **Selfish Motivation:** Acting solely for personal gratification or ego-enhancement.
3. **The Sense of Doership (Kartṛtva abhimāna):** The ego's mistaken belief that "I am the sole performer of this action," forgetting the interplay of natural forces (Gunas) and divine will.

Krishna teaches that one who is free from dualities like desire and aversion, who is not swayed by personal likes and dislikes, is a true *Nitya Sannyasi* (one who is always a renunciate), even while actively engaged in the world. Such a person performs all actions with their body, mind, intellect, and even senses, but purely for self-purification (*atma-shuddhaye*), without any proprietary claim or selfish attachment. They live like a lotus leaf, which, though resting on water, remains untouched and unwet by it.

This inner detachment allows one to perform their *Dharma* (duties) effectively and peacefully. You can be a dedicated professional, a loving family member, or an active contributor to society, yet maintain an inner sanctuary of calm and freedom by renouncing the ego's claim over actions and their fruits. This approach makes spiritual life accessible not just to hermits, but to everyone engaged in the daily activities of life. It's about transforming your engagement with the world from a source of bondage to a means of liberation.

Leadership Lessons in Detachment: Case Studies of Leaders (Indian Context) Who Practiced Effective Detachment

Effective leadership often requires making difficult decisions for the greater good, navigating complex situations, and inspiring others, all while managing personal pressures. Leaders who cultivate detachment often demonstrate remarkable wisdom, resilience, and ethical fortitude.

Emperor Ashoka: After the bloody Kalinga war, Ashoka was overwhelmed by remorse at the immense suffering caused by his ambition. His subsequent transformation involved a profound shift in his approach to kingship. While he didn't abandon his royal duties, he renounced aggressive warfare and dedicated his reign to the welfare of his people, promoting peace, social justice, and religious tolerance through his edicts. His later life exemplified ruling with a sense of detached responsibility and a focus on *Dharma* rather than personal glory or expansionism.

Raja Janaka: A revered king in ancient Indian tradition, Janaka was renowned as a *Videha* (one without body-consciousness or attachment to the physical) and a self-realized sage, even while expertly ruling his kingdom. He actively participated in worldly affairs, fulfilled all his royal duties, and engaged in philosophical discourse, yet remained internally detached from his power, possessions, and even his own body. He serves as a classic example of a *Karma Sannyasi* – one who lives free while fully engaged.

Modern Ethical Leaders (Conceptual Example): Consider contemporary leaders in business or social sectors who prioritize ethical practices, long-term sustainability, and stakeholder well-being over short-term personal gains or ego-driven expansion. Such leaders often make difficult choices that may not be immediately popular but are rooted in principle. Their ability to do so often stems from a degree of detachment from purely financial outcomes or personal accolades, allowing them to focus on purpose and integrity.

These examples illustrate that detachment is not indifference or inaction. It is a powerful inner stance that allows for clear-sighted, principled, and effective engagement with responsibilities, free from the distortions of ego and selfish desire.

Cultivating Inner Freedom: Techniques for Mindful Awareness & Selective Inaction

Inner freedom, the essence of Karma Sanyasa Yoga, can be cultivated through conscious practice:

1. **Mindful Awareness (Sakshi Bhava – The Witness Attitude):** This involves developing the capacity to observe your thoughts, emotions, sensations, and urges without immediately identifying with them or reacting to them. When you feel a strong desire, a surge of anger, or a wave of anxiety, practice stepping back internally and just noticing it: "Ah, there is desire arising," or "There is anger present." This creates a crucial space between the stimulus and your response, allowing you to choose a considered action rather than a knee-jerk reaction. This witnessing helps you realize you are not your thoughts or emotions, but the awareness observing them.

2. **Observing the Ego's Play:** Become familiar with the voice and patterns of your ego – its need for validation, its fear of criticism, its tendency to claim credit for successes and blame others for failures, its constant craving for more. By observing these patterns, you begin to loosen their grip. You can start to see the ego's demands as just another set of thoughts, not as your fundamental truth.

3. **Understanding True Doership:** The Gita teaches that actions are ultimately performed by the interplay of the Gunas (the modes of material nature). While we experience ourselves as acting, a deeper understanding reveals that our individual self

(Atman) is the silent witness, not the ultimate doer. Contemplating this helps reduce the burden of "I must make this happen" & anxiety of "What if I fail?"

4. **Selective Inaction (Strategic Letting Go):** While diligent action is important, Karma Sanyasa Yoga also involves the wisdom of knowing when *not* to act, especially if the impulse comes from ego, anger, greed, or overwhelming attachment. Sometimes, stepping back, allowing a situation to unfold, or choosing silence over a reactive comment is the most powerful and detached "action." This isn't about passivity or laziness, but a conscious, discerning choice to refrain from actions that would create further agitation or negative karma.

These practices gradually shift your identification from the ever-changing drama of the mind and world to the calm, stable center of awareness within, fostering true inner freedom even amidst activity.

Discerning Action: Knowing When to Act Decisively vs. When to Let Go

Living as a Karma Sannyasi requires *Viveka* – clear discernment. How do we know if our actions are aligned with Dharma and detachment, or if they are driven by ego and attachment? How do we decide when to push forward and when to gracefully let go?

Consider these guidelines:

Motivation Check:

Action likely aligned with Dharma/Detachment: Is the primary motivation a sense of duty, service, contributing to a larger good, or expressing your true nature and skills constructively? Does it feel "right" at a deep, intuitive level, even if difficult? Is there a sense of calm resolve?

Action likely ego-driven/attached: Is the motivation primarily personal gain, proving a point, seeking praise, avoiding blame, fear of loss, envy, anger, or a desperate need to control the outcome? Is there a strong emotional charge, agitation, or obsession?

Focus of Attention:

Detached Action: Is your focus primarily on performing the action to the best of your ability, with skill and integrity, letting the results unfold as they may?

Attached Action: Is your mind obsessively fixated on the desired outcome, constantly calculating chances of success/failure, or worrying about what others will think?

Inner State During/After Action:

Detached Action: Leads to a sense of inner satisfaction from having done your part, regardless of the outcome. There's a capacity to learn from setbacks without being crushed.

Attached Action: Leads to intense elation/ego inflation with success, and deep frustration/despair with failure. Peace of mind is entirely dependent on external results.

Considering the Greater Good: Does the action consider the well-being of others and the broader context, or is it narrowly self-serving, potentially at the expense of others or ethical principles?

Effort vs. Outcome: Sometimes, despite our best efforts performed with the right intention, desired outcomes don't materialize due to factors beyond our control. Discernment involves recognizing when we have done all that we reasonably can, and then gracefully letting go of the outcome without bitterness or prolonged struggle. This isn't giving up, but wisely accepting the limits of personal agency.

Developing this discernment is an ongoing practice. It involves honest self-reflection, listening to your purified intuition (the "still, small voice within"), and sometimes seeking guidance from wise counsel.

Chapter 5 Takeaway: Freedom in Action, Peace in Engagement

Karma Sanyasa Yoga brilliantly resolves the apparent conflict between action and renunciation. It teaches that true freedom is not found by escaping the world or our responsibilities, but by transforming our inner approach to them. By performing our duties with skill and dedication, while renouncing attachment to the fruits of our actions and the egoistic sense of doership, we engage with life fully, yet remain inwardly free and untouched, like the lotus leaf. This path allows us to find profound peace, purpose, and even joy, not *despite* our actions, but *through* them. It is the art of living in the world with wisdom, contributing meaningfully without being bound by the inevitable drama of outcomes.

ब्रह्मण्याधाय कर्माणि सङ्गं त्यक्त्वा करोति यः । लिप्यते न स पापेन पद्मपत्रमिवाम्भसा ॥ ५.१० ॥

**Brahmaṇy-ādhāya karmāṇi saṅgaṁ tyaktvā karoti yaḥ |
Lipyate na sa pāpena padma-patram-ivāmbhasā || 5.10 ||**

Hindi: "जो व्यक्ति कर्मफलों में आसक्ति त्यागकर, सब कर्म ब्रह्म को अर्पण करके करता है, वह जल में कमल के पत्ते की तरह पाप से लिप्त नहीं होता।"

English: "One who performs his duty without attachment, surrendering the results unto the Supreme Lord, is unaffected by sinful action, as the lotus leaf is untouched by water." ***(This verse beautifully encapsulates the principle of detached action.)***

Exercise: Discerning Your Actions – A Reflection on Engagement and Letting Go

This exercise helps you apply the principles of discernment discussed in this chapter to a current situation in your life where you might be unsure whether to act decisively, modify your approach, or practice letting go.

Identify a Current Situation: Choose a situation, decision, or area of your life where you feel a pull to act, or perhaps where you are already acting but feel conflicted, stressed, or overly attached to the outcome. (e.g., A challenging project at work, a difficult family dynamic, a personal goal you're striving for, a community issue you're involved in).

Examine Your Motivation: Reflect honestly on *why* you want to act or are acting in this situation.

- What are your primary drivers? (e.g., Sense of duty, desire for a specific outcome, fear of consequences if you don't act, need for approval, personal gain, service to others).
- Is there a strong emotional charge (anger, fear, excitement, anxiety) fueling your desire to act? How much of it is ego-driven ("I need to prove...", "I want to control...")?

Assess Your Attachment to the Outcome:

- How important is a *specific* result to you? What are you hoping to achieve?
- How would you feel if the outcome was different from desired (e.g.failure, no recognition, a different result)? How intense would your reaction be?
- Are you able to focus on performing the action well, irrespective of the exact outcome, or is your mind constantly fixated on the future result?

Consider the 'Dharma' Aspect:

- Does this action feel aligned with your core values and responsibilities (your Svadharma)?

- Does it contribute positively to yourself and others, or to a larger good?

Weigh Decisive Action vs. Letting Go:

- **Case for Decisive Action:** What are the indicators that firm, continued, or new action is needed? (e.g., A clear duty, a problem that will worsen without intervention, an opportunity that requires effort).
- **Case for Modifying Action/Letting Go (of specific outcomes or the entire effort):** What are the indicators that perhaps your current approach needs changing, or that it's time to step back or accept things as they are? (e.g., Exhausting all reasonable efforts with no positive movement due to external factors, actions driven by unhealthy attachment/ego, recognizing the situation is beyond your control, realizing the cost of continued effort outweighs potential benefits).

Formulate a 'Detached Action Plan' or 'Wise Letting Go' Strategy:

Based on your reflections, what would it look like to engage in this situation with greater detachment? If action is needed, how can you perform it as your duty & focusing on skillful execution for optimum results?

If letting go (of a specific outcome, or the effort itself) seems wiser, what would that involve? How can you do so with peace and acceptance, rather than resentment or defeat?

What small step can you take today to practice this more detached engagement or wise letting go?

(This reflective exercise helps you move from reactive behavior to conscious, discerned action or inaction, cultivating inner freedom even as you navigate the complexities of life.)

Adhyay 6: Master Your Mind – Your Simple Guide to Inner Peace & Unshakeable Calm

(Atma Samyama Yoga / Dhyana Yoga – The Yoga of Self-Control / Meditation)

The Unruly Mind: Taming Your Inner Chariot

In the preceding chapters, Krishna has illuminated profound paths: understanding our true Self (Sankhya Yoga), acting selflessly (Karma Yoga), embracing transformative knowledge (Jnana Yoga), and living with detached engagement (Karma Sanyasa Yoga). These paths, while distinct, all lead towards inner freedom and purposeful living. However, a common thread runs through them all: the undeniable necessity of a calm, controlled, and focused mind. Without some mastery over our own mental turbulence, trying to implement these profound teachings can feel like trying to navigate a storm in a rudderless boat.

Arjuna himself voices this challenge, famously comparing the mind to the wind – restless, turbulent, strong, and incredibly difficult to control. Krishna acknowledges this difficulty but asserts that it *can* be achieved through consistent practice (*Abhyasa*) and detachment (*Vairagya*). This chapter, Atma Samyama Yoga (often referred to as

Dhyana Yoga), delves into the art and science of meditation – the practical toolkit for taming the unruly mind, achieving inner stillness, and directly experiencing the truths previously discussed. Mastering the mind is the key to unlocking lasting peace and unshakable calm.

Your Meditation Toolkit: Simple Techniques for Focus & Mindfulness

Meditation, at its core, is a practice of training attention and cultivating a specific kind of awareness. Its purpose is to quiet the incessant chatter of the mind, enhance concentration, deepen self-understanding, and ultimately, enable us to connect with our true, peaceful Self (Atman). While there are many techniques, the Gita emphasizes a disciplined yet gentle approach.

Setting the Stage for Meditation (as per the Gita): Krishna offers practical advice for creating a conducive environment:

- **A Suitable Place:** Choose a clean, quiet, and secluded spot where you are unlikely to be disturbed.
- **A Firm Seat:** Prepare a seat that is neither too high nor too low, traditionally made of kusha grass, covered with a deerskin (or a soft cloth/blanket for modern practitioners), ensuring it is firm and comfortable.
- **Steady Posture:** Sit with the body, head, and neck erect and still. A comfortable, stable posture is key

(e.g., cross-legged on the floor if comfortable, or upright in a chair with feet flat).

- **Moderation in Habits:** The Gita emphasizes the importance of regulating food, sleep, work, and recreation for one whose goal is to practice yoga effectively. Extremes are to be avoided.

Core Meditation Techniques:

1. **Breath Awareness (Anapana Sati):** This is one of the most accessible and foundational techniques.

How: Simply bring your gentle, non-judgmental attention to the natural sensation of your breath. You might focus on the tip of your nostrils, feeling the air enter and leave, or on the rise and fall of your abdomen. There's no need to control or change your breath; just observe its natural rhythm.

Benefit: Focusing on the breath anchors the mind in the present moment, calming its tendency to wander into past regrets or future anxieties. It builds concentration and tranquility.

2. **Single-Pointed Focus (Ekagrata):**

How: Direct your attention to a single, chosen object of focus. This could be:

- A visual object (with eyes gently closed or softly gazing): A mental image of a calming symbol (like 'Om' ॐ), a deity, a point of light, or the flame of a candle (if eyes are open).

- An auditory object: The mental repetition of a mantra (a sacred sound or phrase, like 'Om', or a longer mantra if you have one from a tradition).
- A specific sensation: The feeling of the breath, as above, or a subtle internal sensation.

Benefit: This practice trains the mind to remain steady and one-pointed, significantly enhancing concentration and reducing mental distractions.

3. **Mindfulness of Thoughts & Emotions (Witnessing Awareness):**

How: As introduced in earlier exercises, this involves becoming a detached observer of your own mental content. Allow thoughts, feelings, memories, and sensations to arise and pass through your awareness without getting caught up in them, analyzing them, or judging them. Simply note their presence: "A thought of work is arising," "A feeling of restlessness is here," and let them go.

Benefit: This practice helps you disidentify from your mental chatter, realizing that you are not your thoughts or emotions, but the spacious awareness in which they occur. This creates inner freedom and reduces reactivity.

Key Principles for Practice:

- **Start Simple & Short:** Begin with 5-10 mins daily and gradually increase the duration.

- **Consistency Over Intensity:** Regular daily practice is more effective than long, infrequent sessions.

- **Gentle Persistence:** The mind *will* wander – that's its nature. The practice is not to prevent wandering, but to gently and patiently bring your attention back to your chosen focus each time it strays, without self-criticism.

The Science of Zen: Proven Benefits of Meditation for a Busy Life

The "Zen" state – one of calm, focused awareness – isn't just a spiritual aspiration; its pursuit through meditation has been increasingly validated by modern science for its profound benefits, making it an invaluable tool for navigating our busy, often stressful, modern lives.

Stress Reduction & Resilience: Numerous studies show that regular meditation helps regulate the body's stress response. It can lower levels of the stress hormone cortisol, calm the sympathetic nervous system (our "fight-or-flight" mode), and activate the parasympathetic nervous system (our "rest-and-digest" mode). This builds greater emotional resilience to life's pressures.

Improved Focus & Attention Span: In our age of constant digital distraction, the ability to concentrate is a superpower. Meditation, especially focus-based techniques, strengthens the brain's prefrontal cortex, which is crucial for attention, working memory, and executive function. This can translate to better productivity and clarity in your work and studies.

Emotional Regulation & Well-being: Meditation cultivates self-awareness and creates a crucial "pause button" between an emotional trigger and our reaction. This allows us to respond more thoughtfully rather than react impulsively to difficult emotions like anger, anxiety, or sadness. It's associated with increased positive emotions and overall life satisfaction.

Cognitive Benefits: Some research suggests meditation can enhance cognitive flexibility, creativity, and even slow down age-related cognitive decline by promoting brain health.

Physical Health Contributions: While not a cure-all, meditation has been linked to ancillary physical benefits such as lower blood pressure, improved sleep quality (by calming the mind before bed), and even a strengthened immune response by reducing chronic stress.

Enhanced Self-Awareness & Introspection: By regularly turning inward, meditation helps us understand our own mental habits, conditioned patterns, biases, and emotional triggers more clearly. This self-knowledge is the foundation for personal growth and transforming unhelpful patterns.

These scientifically-backed benefits make meditation a highly practical tool for anyone seeking to improve their mental, emotional and physical well-being in the face of modern life's demands, especially in high-pressure urban environments where stress can be a significant factor.

Build Your Calm Habit: A Step-by-Step Plan for Daily Meditation That Sticks

Knowing the benefits of meditation is one thing; establishing a consistent practice is another. Here's a simple plan to help you build a sustainable meditation habit:

1. **Commit to a Tiny Start:** Begin with just 5 or 10 minutes a day. The goal is to make it so easy that you can't say no. You can always increase the duration later once the habit is formed.

2. **Choose a Consistent Time & Place:** Try to meditate at roughly the same time each day to help automate the behavior. Early morning, before the day's demands begin, works well for many, or perhaps in the evening to unwind. Find a quiet spot where you're unlikely to be interrupted.

3. **Prepare Your Space (Optional but helpful):** Keep your meditation space clean and inviting. You might have a specific cushion or chair you use. This creates a ritualistic element that can support the habit.

4. **Set a Gentle Reminder:** Use your phone or a calendar reminder until the habit becomes ingrained.

5. **Just Show Up (Especially on Difficult Days):** There will be days when you don't feel like meditating, or when your mind feels particularly restless. On these days, just sitting for a few minutes, even if it feels "unsuccessful," reinforces the habit. The act of showing up is a victory in itself.

6. **Be Patient and Non-Judgmental:** This is crucial. Your mind *will* wander. You'll have "good" days and "distracted" days. This is normal. The practice isn't about achieving a perfectly silent mind immediately, but about patiently and kindly returning your

attention to your chosen focus each time it strays. Avoid self-criticism.

7. **Anchor it to an Existing Habit (Habit Stacking):** Link your meditation practice to something you already do daily, like after your morning tea/coffee, or before you brush your teeth at night. This makes it easier to remember.

8. **Reflect Briefly (Optional):** You might spend a minute after your session noticing how you feel, or occasionally journal about your experiences, challenges, and insights. This can provide encouragement.

9. **Extend Mindfulness Beyond Formal Sitting:** Gradually try to bring the qualities cultivated in meditation – awareness, presence, non-judgment – into your daily activities: mindful eating, mindful walking, mindful listening. This integrates the practice into your life.

Building any new habit takes time and consistent effort. Approach meditation with a spirit of gentle discipline and self-compassion, and the benefits will gradually unfold.

Chapter 6 Takeaway: Your Mind, Your Ally

The mind can be our greatest obstacle or our most powerful ally on the path to peace and self-realization. Atma Samyama Yoga, the path of meditation and self-control, provides the practical means to transform the mind from a source of agitation and distraction into an instrument of clarity, focus, and profound inner stillness. By consistently practicing the techniques outlined, even for a short duration each day, you begin to quiet the mental chatter, understand your inner landscape more deeply, and cultivate an unshakeable calm that allows you to navigate life's challenges with greater wisdom and equanimity. Mastering your mind is not about suppressing it, but about understanding it and befriending it, so it can reflect the peace and brilliance of your true Self.

शनैः शनैरुपरमेद् बुद्ध्या धृतगृहीतया । आत्मसंस्थं मनः कृत्वा न किञ्चिदपि चिन्तयेत् ॥ ६.२५ ॥

Śanaiḥ śanair-uparamed buddhyā dhṛiti-gṛihītayā | Ātma-saṁsthaṁ manaḥ kṛitvā na kiñchid-api chintayet || 6.25 ||

Hindi: "धैर्ययुक्त बुद्धि के द्वारा धीरे-धीरे अभ्यास करते हुए उपरति को प्राप्त हो तथा मन को आत्मा में स्थित करके अन्य कुछ भी चिन्तन न करे।"

English: "Gradually, step by step, one should become situated in trance by means of intelligence sustained by conviction, and thus the mind should be fixed on the Self alone and should think of nothing else." ***(This verse describes the gradual process of steadying the mind in meditation.)***

Exercise: Seeds of Stillness – Guided Meditation & Reflection

This section offers ideas for guided meditation and reflective activities to help you cultivate self-control and deepen your connection with inner calm.

1. Guided Meditation Idea: Calm Abiding (10-Minute Script Outline)

- **(0-1 min) Settling In:** "Find a comfortable, upright posture... Gently close your eyes... Take three slow, deep breaths, releasing tension with each exhale..."
- **(1-3 min) Body Scan Awareness:** "Bring your awareness to the sensations in your body... Notice your feet on the floor... your seat... your hands... Scan upwards, noticing any areas of tension... Simply acknowledge them without judgment..."
- **(3-7 min) Breath Focus:** "Now, gently bring your attention to your breath... Notice the natural rhythm... the cool air entering... the warm air leaving... Don't try to change it... just observe... If your mind wanders, gently guide it back to the breath..."
- **(7-9 min) Resting in Stillness:** "Let go of focusing on the breath... Simply rest in the awareness of this present moment... a sense of calm, stillness... If thoughts arise, let them pass like clouds..."
- **(9-10 min) Gentle Return:** "Gradually deepen your breath... Become aware of your body again... your

surroundings... When you're ready, slowly open your eyes... Carry this sense of calm with you."

2. Guided Meditation Idea: Witnessing Thoughts (10-Minute Script Outline)

- **(0-1 min) Settling In:** (Similar to above)
- **(1-3 min) Breath Anchor:** "Begin by resting your attention on your breath for a few moments, allowing the mind to settle..."
- **(3-8 min) Observing Thoughts:** "Now, shift your awareness to your thoughts... Imagine you are sitting by the side of a gently flowing stream, and your thoughts are like leaves floating by... Don't try to grab them or analyze them... Simply notice them as they appear... pass... and disappear... Label them gently if you wish: 'thinking,' 'planning,' 'remembering'... Maintain your position as the detached observer..."
- **(8-9 min) Resting as the Witness:** "Recognize that you are the awareness that is watching the thoughts... not the thoughts themselves... Rest in this spacious, witnessing presence..."
- **(9-10 min) Gentle Return:** (Similar to above)

3. Reflective Exercises for Deepening Self-Control:

To deepen your self-control, consider reflecting on one or two of the following ideas in your journal:

- "Identify one specific area in your daily life where you often feel reactive or lose your composure (e.g., traffic jams, a particular interaction, when plans change suddenly). How could consistently practicing a short daily meditation begin to create more 'space' for a calmer response in these situations?"

- "What is the biggest obstacle you perceive in establishing or maintaining a regular meditation practice? What is one small, practical step you can take this week to address this obstacle and support your intention to meditate?"

- "Recall a recent instance where you successfully exercised self-control over an unhelpful impulse or emotion. What inner resources or thought processes helped you in that moment? How can the awareness cultivated in meditation further strengthen these resources?"

- "The Gita mentions *Abhyasa* (consistent practice) and *Vairagya* (detachment/dispassion) as keys to controlling the mind. How do you understand these two principles in the context of your own efforts to cultivate inner calm and self-mastery? Where can you apply them more consciously?"

(Remember, these practices are like planting seeds. With consistent, patient nurturing, they will gradually grow into a strong inner tree of calm, clarity, and self-mastery.)

Part II: Integrate Wisdom – Transform How You Live (Adhyays 7-12)

Having established the foundations in Part I – understanding the nature of the Self, the importance of selfless action, the power of knowledge, the art of detachment, and the necessity of mind control – we now embark on a deeper exploration. Part II of our journey delves into integrating this wisdom more fully into our being and our daily lives. Krishna begins to reveal more about the ultimate reality, His own divine nature, and the various paths through which we can connect with and realize this truth directly. These chapters guide us from intellectual understanding towards profound, lived experience, transforming not just what we know, but how we perceive the world and live within it.

Adhyay 7: From Knowing to Being – Make Wisdom Your Lived Reality

(Gyaan Vigyana Yoga – The Yoga of Knowledge and Realization)

Bridging Knowledge and Experience

The journey so far has equipped us with essential tools and understanding. We've explored the nature of our inner battlefield (Adhyay 1), the distinction between the eternal Self and the temporary body (Adhyay 2), the path of selfless action (Adhyay 3), the purifying power of knowledge (Adhyay 4), the freedom found in detached engagement (Adhyay 5), and the methods for mastering the mind through meditation (Adhyay 6). Now, Krishna takes us a crucial step further. He begins to unveil the difference between simply *knowing* about these truths intellectually (*Gyaan*) and directly *experiencing* and *living* them as our reality (*Vigyana*).

Gyaan Vigyana Yoga is the yoga that bridges this gap. It's about moving beyond theoretical understanding to profound, intuitive realization. It requires not just accumulating information but assimilating wisdom so deeply that it transforms our perception and permeates our very being. In this chapter, Krishna starts revealing His own supreme nature as the underlying reality behind both the material and spiritual worlds, offering knowledge that, when realized, leads to complete liberation.

Beyond Theory: Merging Intellectual Understanding (Gyaan) with Direct Experience (Vigyana)

Imagine the difference between reading an incredibly detailed map of Mumbai (*Gyaan*) and actually navigating its bustling streets, experiencing its sights, sounds, and energy firsthand (*Vigyana*). Or consider the difference between knowing the chemical formula for water (*Gyaan*) and feeling the refreshment of drinking a cool glass on a hot day (*Vigyana*).

- **Gyaan (ज्ञान):** This is conceptual knowledge. It's the understanding we gain through study, listening to teachers, logical reasoning, and intellectual analysis. We might understand, for example, "I am not this physical body; I am the eternal Atman." This knowledge is crucial – it provides the map, the framework. It helps us discriminate between the real and the unreal.

- **Vigyana (विज्ञान):** This is realized knowledge, wisdom born from direct experience and deep inner conviction. It's when intellectual understanding becomes a lived reality. Continuing the example, *Vigyana* is the state where you *feel* and *live* from the perspective of the eternal Atman, fundamentally free from the anxieties and limitations associated solely with the body and mind. Doubts dissolve not just through logic, but through inner certainty.

Krishna emphasizes that while many may strive for intellectual understanding, truly realizing this knowledge (*Vigyana*) is rare. Why? Because it requires more than just study; it demands purification of the mind (through practices like Karma Yoga and Dhyana Yoga), sincere self-inquiry, and often, divine grace. *Vigyana* integrates head and heart, transforming knowledge *about* the truth into the direct perception *of* the truth. It's this realized wisdom that truly liberates. Krishna himself begins to impart this deeper knowledge by explaining His own energies – the material energy (Prakriti, comprising earth, water, fire, air, ether, mind, intelligence, ego) and the superior spiritual energy (the living entities, Atman) – revealing Himself as the source and sustainer of all that exists.

The Path to Liberation: How Realizing Your True Self Sets You Free

The root cause of our suffering and bondage, as discussed earlier, is *Avidya* – ignorance of our true nature. We mistakenly identify with the temporary, limited self (the body-mind-ego complex) and forget our eternal, unlimited identity as the Atman, intrinsically connected to the Supreme Reality.

Gyaan begins the process of dispelling this ignorance by providing the correct intellectual framework. *Vigyana* completes it by making that understanding unshakable through direct experience. When we fully realize – not just intellectually believe, but experientially *know* – our true nature as the eternal, unchanging, blissful Self (Atman), distinct from the temporary world, the following occurs:

- **Freedom from Fear:** The greatest fear is the fear of death, rooted in identification with the perishable body. Realizing the Self as eternal and indestructible eradicates this fear at its core. Fear of loss, failure, or change also diminishes drastically, as the true Self is inherently secure and unchanging.

- **Freedom from Attachment & Aversion:** Understanding the temporary nature of worldly objects and experiences, and knowing the true source of happiness lies within the Self, naturally reduces desperate clinging (attachment) and intense dislike (aversion). This leads to greater emotional balance and peace.
- **Freedom from Karma:** As highlighted in Adhyay 4, the fire of realized knowledge (Gyaan-Vigyana) burns away the accumulated reactions of past actions and prevents the creation of new binding karma, as actions are performed without selfish motive or attachment.
- **Living in Constant Awareness:** Liberation isn't just a future state after death; it's a state of being that can be experienced here and now. It involves living with the constant background awareness of one's true identity as the eternal observer, the Atman, connected to the Supreme.

This realization isn't merely a passive state of knowing; it fundamentally transforms how we perceive and interact with the world, leading to a life lived with freedom, purpose, and unshakeable inner peace.

Integrating Wisdom Daily: Weaving Knowledge into Everyday Actions

How does this profound realization translate into practical, everyday living? It's not about isolating oneself, but about transforming one's perspective and engagement *within* the world. Krishna provides clues in this chapter:

1. **Seeing the Divine Essence Everywhere:** Krishna declares He is the underlying essence in all of creation: "I am the taste in water, the light in the sun and moon, the syllable Om in the Vedic mantras; I am the sound in ether and ability in man." (BG 7.8, paraphrased). A key practice becomes consciously looking for and appreciating this divine thread woven through all experiences. See the divine energy in the warmth of the sun, the nourishment from food, the intelligence behind technology, the love in relationships. This shifts perception from mundane to sacred.

2. **Action Rooted in Knowledge:** Continue performing your duties (Karma Yoga), but now with the added layer of awareness gained through Gyaan-Vigyana. Understand that the energy to act comes from the Supreme source, and the actions themselves are interactions of the Gunas (material modes). See yourself less as the independent "doer" and more as a conscious instrument acting within a larger divine play. This perspective naturally fosters detachment and humility.

3. **Equanimity Born of Realization:** The inner balance cultivated is no longer just based on tolerance for dualities (like pleasure/pain), but stems from the direct *realization* that your true Self is inherently beyond these fluctuations. Worldly events still happen, but they lose their power to fundamentally disturb your inner peace because your anchor is in the eternal.

4. **Constant Remembrance (Smaranam):** Integrate moments of conscious remembrance of your true Self or the Supreme throughout the day. This could be through silent mantra repetition, brief mindful pauses to reconnect with your inner awareness, or seeing daily activities as an offering. This weaves the thread of wisdom into the fabric of your moment-to-moment experience.

These practices help bridge the gap between understanding the truth and living the truth, making Gyaan-Vigyana a dynamic, transformative path integrated into life itself.

Chapter 7 Takeaway: From Knowing About to Knowing As

Gyaan-Vigyana Yoga marks a crucial deepening of the spiritual path presented in the Gita. It calls us to move beyond simply knowing *about* the eternal Self and the Supreme Reality to directly *knowing* and *experiencing* this truth as our own lived reality. This realized wisdom (Vigyana), built upon the foundation of intellectual knowledge (Gyaan), is the key that unlocks true liberation from fear, attachment, and suffering. By beginning to perceive the divine essence within all of creation and performing actions with this enlightened awareness, we transform our entire experience of life, paving the way for unshakeable peace and freedom.

मनुष्याणां सहस्रेषु कश्चिद्यतति सिद्धये । यततामपि सिद्धानां कश्चिन्मां वेत्ति तत्त्वतः ॥ ७.३ ॥

Manuṣyāṇāṁ sahasreṣu kaśchid yatati siddhaye | Yatatām api siddhānāṁ kaśchin māṁ vetti tattvataḥ || 7.3 ||

Hindi: "हजारों मनुष्यों में से कोई एक सिद्धि के लिए यत्न करता है, और यत्न करने वाले सिद्धों में से भी कोई एक मुझे तत्त्व से जानता है।"

English: "Out of many thousands among men, one may endeavor for perfection, and of those who have achieved perfection, hardly one knows Me in truth." ***(This verse highlights the rarity and preciousness of achieving true, realized knowledge (Vigyana) of the Supreme Reality.)***

Exercise: Practices for Deepening Realization (Gyaan to Vigyana)

This section offers reflective practices and contemplative exercises to help bridge the gap between intellectual understanding (Gyaan) and lived realization (Vigyana).

Mini Case Study Reflections:

Scenario A (Facing Loss): Maya experienced the painful loss of a long-term job she identified with strongly. Initially devastated, she consciously applied the Gyaan: "I am not my job title; my true Self is eternal and unaffected." Through reflection and meditation (Vigyana practices), she began to *feel* a deeper sense of inner stability independent of her professional role, allowing her to navigate the transition with greater peace and openness to new possibilities. *Reflection:* Think of a time you faced loss or setback. How much did your identification with the external situation contribute to your suffering? How might embodying the perspective of the eternal Self change that experience?

Scenario B (Finding Meaning in the Mundane): Rajesh felt his daily commute in Mumbai traffic was a major source of stress and frustration. He started practicing seeing the divine essence (as per BG 7.8) – the energy powering the vehicles, the life within the people, the complex order underlying the apparent chaos. He consciously offered the commute time as a period for internal reflection or mantra. Slowly, his experience shifted from frustration to a detached, almost curious observation, occasionally touched by a sense of interconnectedness. *Reflection:* Choose one routine, perhaps mundane or stressful, part of your day. How could you consciously practice seeing the underlying divine energy or using that time as an offering or practice in awareness?

Practice: Contemplating the Divine Essence

Choose one element Krishna mentions He is the essence of (e.g., the taste of water, the light of the sun/moon, the sound in ether, the ability in humans, the fragrance of the earth - refer BG 7.8-7.11).

Spend 5-10 minutes consciously interacting with or contemplating this element.

- If water, drink it slowly, focusing purely on the sensation of taste and refreshment. Reflect: Krishna says "He is this taste."
- If sunlight, feel its warmth on your skin. Reflect: "This life-giving energy, this light – Krishna says "He is this light."
- If sound, listen intently to the ambient sounds around you, or the sound of 'Om'. Reflect: "This vibration, this principle of sound – Krishna is this."

The goal isn't intellectual analysis, but to use the senses and contemplation to cultivate a *feeling* or intuitive sense of the divine presence permeating the seemingly ordinary.

Practice: Action in Awareness

Select one simple activity you will do today (e.g., preparing a meal, walking, having a conversation, working on a specific task).

Before starting, set the intention: "I will perform this action with awareness, remembering that the energy to act comes from the Supreme, and my true Self is the silent witness."

During the activity, try to maintain a gentle background awareness of this intention. When you notice yourself getting lost in the action or identifying strongly as the "doer"

("*I* am doing this so well/poorly"), gently remind yourself of the witness perspective.

Don't strive for perfection; simply practice introducing this awareness into activity. Notice any shifts in how you feel while performing the task.

(These practices are subtle yet profound. They require consistent, gentle effort to shift ingrained habits of perception. Be patient and persistent in weaving this deeper awareness into your life.)

Adhyay 8: Your Eternal Anchor – Connecting with the Unchanging Reality

(Akshara Brahma Yoga – The Yoga of the Imperishable Absolute)

Quest for the Ultimate: Arjuna's Fundamental Questions

In Adhyay 7, Krishna began to unveil His supreme nature as the underlying reality of both the material and spiritual worlds, distinguishing between intellectual knowledge (*Gyaan*) and realized wisdom (*Vigyana*). This profound revelation leads Arjuna... to ask a series of fundamental questions. He seeks to understand core metaphysical concepts: What is Brahman (the Absolute)? What is Adhyatma (the individual self)? What is Karma (fruitive activities)? What is Adhibhuta (the material manifestation)? What is Adhidaiva (the universal form of God, or the demigods)? And crucially, Arjuna asks, how can those in devotional service know the Supreme Lord (Adhiyajna, the Lord of sacrifice) at the time of death?

These questions are not mere academic inquiries; they reflect a deep human yearning to understand our place in the cosmos, the nature of ultimate reality, and how to navigate life and death with wisdom. Krishna's answers in this chapter form the essence of *Akshara Brahma Yoga* – the yoga of connecting with the imperishable, unmanifested Absolute (Brahman). This chapter provides us with an "eternal anchor," helping us find stability and purpose in a constantly changing world, especially as we contemplate life's ultimate transition.

The Immortal Soul: Contemplating the Eternal, Imperishable Nature of Your True Self (Atman)

Krishna begins His response by defining some of these key terms. He identifies **Brahman** as the indestructible, transcendental, eternal, and unchangeable principle. He then explains that **Adhyatma** refers to the individual living entity's true spiritual nature – the eternal soul, the *Atman*, which is essentially one in quality with Brahman.

We revisited the nature of the Atman in Adhyay 2 – its eternality, its indestructibility, its unchanging essence beyond the temporary physical body. Here, the contemplation deepens: What does it truly *mean* to live with the constant awareness of being this immortal soul, temporarily housed in a perishable form? How does this understanding fundamentally shift our daily fears, anxieties, attachments, and our perception of life's purpose?

When we begin to internalize that our core identity is not the fleeting body or the shifting mind, but this spark of eternal consciousness (Atman), much of what troubles us loses its power. The fear of personal annihilation dissolves. The desperate clinging to temporary possessions, roles, or relationships lessens, because we recognize that our true Self is inherently complete and beyond these external trappings. This realization of ourselves as the immortal soul, the Adhyatma, is the foundational step toward understanding and connecting with the *Akshara Brahman*, the supreme imperishable reality, which is our ultimate anchor.

Dealing with Impermanence: Philosophical Insights and Scientific Perspectives on Navigating Change

A core theme that underscores the importance of an "eternal anchor" is the pervasive nature of impermanence (*Anityatva*) in the material world. Everything we perceive through our senses is subject to change, decay, and eventual dissolution.

Philosophical Insights: Throughout history, philosophers and spiritual traditions worldwide have emphasized the importance of understanding and accepting impermanence as a key to inner peace.

- **Buddhism,** for example, lists impermanence (Anicca) as one of the fundamental marks of existence. Attachment to impermanent things is seen as a primary cause of suffering.
- **Stoic philosophy** in the West also encouraged recognizing what is within our control versus what is not, and accepting the transient nature of external events with equanimity. The Gita teaches that while the material world (*Adhibhuta* – the physical manifestation, which is constantly changing) is impermanent, the spirit (Atman/Brahman) is eternal. Developing wisdom involves differentiating between these two and anchoring oneself in the eternal.

Scientific Echoes (Accessible Perspectives): While science and spirituality explore reality through different methodologies, some scientific observations resonate with the philosophical understanding of impermanence:

- **The Second Law of Thermodynamics (Entropy):** In physics, this law describes the natural tendency of isolated systems to move towards increasing disorder and decay over time. It reflects a fundamental directionality of change in the physical universe.
- **Cosmology & Astrophysics:** Our understanding of the universe reveals constant flux – stars are born and die, galaxies evolve, and the universe itself is expanding and changing. Krishna also describes cosmic cycles of manifestation and dissolution of universes.
- **Biology & Life Cycles:** All living organisms undergo cycles of birth, growth, reproduction, decay, and death. Our own bodies are in a state of constant cellular turnover; the body you have today is not the same as the one you had years ago, nor the one you will have in the future.

These perspectives, whether ancient philosophy or modern science, highlight the ever-changing nature of the phenomenal world. This understanding isn't meant to be pessimistic, but realistic. It encourages us to seek something more stable and enduring to base our sense of self and security upon. If everything around us and even our physical form is constantly changing, where can we find an unshakeable anchor? The Gita answers: in the eternal Self (Atman) and its connection to the Imperishable Absolute (Akshara Brahman).

Connection Practices: Techniques Designed to Help You Connect with Your Unchanging Core Self

Krishna provides crucial guidance on how to connect with this unchanging reality, particularly emphasizing the state of consciousness at the time of death. He states unequivocally:

"Whatever state of being one remembers when he quits his body, O son of Kuntī, that state he will attain without fail." (BG 8.6, paraphrased)

This profound statement underscores the importance of our predominant thoughts and consciousness throughout life, as these will naturally shape our focus at the critical moment of leaving the body. Therefore, connecting with our eternal anchor is not just a deathbed practice, but a lifelong endeavor.

Key Practices for Connection:

Constant Remembrance (Smaranam / Chintana): The most emphasized practice in this chapter is the continuous remembrance of the Supreme Lord or the eternal Self.

- **Mantra Japa:** Regular, focused repetition of sacred sounds or names of the Divine (like 'Om', or specific mantras like 'Hare Krishna' or 'Sri Ram'). This helps to purify the mind & keep us focused on the spiritual.

- **Contemplation & Meditation on the Absolute:** Devoting time daily to meditate on the nature of the Atman, Brahman, or the personal form of the God (as Krishna begins to reveal Himself). This involves focusing the mind & intellect on the spiritual truths.

- **Offering Daily Actions:** As an extension of Karma Yoga, consciously performing all actions as an offering to the Supreme, remembering Him as the ultimate enjoyer and controller. This infuses daily life with spiritual awareness.

Chanting 'Om' (ॐ) and Remembering the Lord: Krishna specifically mentions that one who, at the time of death, vibrates the sacred syllable 'Om' (which represents Brahman) and remembers Him, attains the supreme destination.

Disciplined Life: A life of regulated senses, a mind consistently engaged in thoughts of the Divine, and an intellect fixed on the Supreme (as described in Adhyay 6) naturally facilitates this remembrance. This includes moderation in daily habits – eating, sleeping, recreation – which helps maintain mental clarity and focus.

Devotional Service (Bhakti Yoga): While Bhakti Yoga will be detailed later, Krishna introduces the concept that those who constantly engage in His devotional service with love and determination easily attain Him.

The goal of these practices is to make the consciousness of our eternal nature and our connection to the Supreme so deeply ingrained that it becomes our natural state, ensuring that at the critical juncture of death, our thoughts are fixed on the eternal, thus leading us to the eternal.

Chapter 8 Takeaway: Anchored in the Eternal Amidst Change

Akshara Brahma Yoga provides profound reassurance: amidst the undeniable impermanence of the material world, there exists an eternal, unchanging reality – Brahman, and our own true Self, the Atman, is an inseparable part of it. By understanding this truth and diligently practicing the art of remembrance – integrating awareness of the eternal into our daily lives and thoughts – we can find an unshakeable anchor. This not only helps us navigate life's changes and challenges with greater peace and fearlessness but also determines our ultimate destination. The key is consistent, lifelong practice aimed at purifying our consciousness and fixing our minds on the Supreme.

अन्तकाले च मामेव स्मरन्मुक्त्वा कलेवरम् । यः प्रयाति स मद्भावं याति नास्त्यत्र संशयः ॥ ८.५ ॥

Anta-kāle ca mām-eva smaran muktvā kalevaram | Yaḥ prayāti sa mad-bhāvaṁ yāti nāsty-atra saṁśayaḥ || 8.5 ||

Hindi: "और अन्तकाल में भी मेरा ही स्मरण करते हुए शरीर को त्यागकर जो जाता है, वह मेरे भाव को प्राप्त होता है; इसमें कोई संशय नहीं है।"

English: "And whoever, at the end of his life, quits his body remembering Me alone, at once attains My nature. Of this there is no doubt." *(This verse highlights the critical importance of remembering the Supreme at the time of death.)*

Exercise: Reflective Insights and Practices to Internalize Your Eternal Nature

These exercises are designed to help you deepen your understanding of impermanence and cultivate a connection with your unchanging, eternal Self.

1. **Reflection on Impermanence & Change:**

Exercise: Take a few moments to reflect on two or three things in your life that you once considered stable or permanent but which have significantly changed or are no longer present (e.g., a past job, a relationship, a physical ability, a cherished possession, a phase of life).

Journal: Describe these changes briefly. How did you feel when these changes occurred? What did you learn from navigating them? How might an awareness of your "eternal anchor" – your unchanging true Self – have altered your experience or response to these changes?

2. **Contemplating Your Core Self:**

Exercise: Find a quiet moment and sit comfortably. Gently bring to mind the various roles you play in life (e.g., professional, son/daughter, parent, friend, etc.), your possessions, your physical body, your thoughts, and your emotions.

Journal/Reflection: Ask yourself: "If all these roles, possessions, and even this body were to change or disappear, what would remain? Who is the 'I' that is aware of all these changing aspects?" Don't search for an intellectual answer, but rather try to get a *sense* of the unchanging awareness that underlies all your experiences. Journal any insights or feelings that arise.

3. **Practice: Mantra or Affirmation for Remembrance:**

Choose: Select a short, sacred mantra (like "Om," "So Hum," or a name of the Divine that resonates with you) or a simple affirmation (e.g., "I am eternal awareness," "My true Self is peace," "I am anchored in the unchanging").

Practice: For 5-10 minutes, sit quietly and repeat your chosen mantra or affirmation silently or in a very soft whisper. Let the sound and meaning fill your mind. If your mind wanders, gently bring it back. The aim is to create a resonance with the idea of your eternal nature.

4. **Practice: Moments of Conscious Remembrance:**

Set an Intention: Decide to consciously remember your "eternal anchor" or the presence of the Supreme for just one minute, at three specific, pre-decided times during your day (e.g., upon waking, before a meal, midday, before sleep).

During the Minute: Pause whatever you are doing. Close your eyes if possible. Take a deep breath and bring to mind your chosen mantra, affirmation, or simply the feeling of your unchanging inner presence or the presence of the

Divine.

Notice: Observe any subtle shift in your state of mind or your perspective after this brief moment of conscious remembrance.

(Internalizing the truth of your eternal nature is a gradual process. Consistent reflection and practice help to shift your identification from the fleeting to the everlasting, bringing profound peace and stability.)

Adhyay 9: Unlock Life's Deepest Secrets – Tap Into Your Hidden Potential

(Raja Vidya Raja Guhya Yoga – The Yoga of Royal Knowledge and the Most Confidential Secret)

The King of Knowledge: A Revelation of Profound Truth

Having explored the nature of the imperishable Absolute (Brahman) and the importance of constant remembrance in Adhyay 8, Lord Krishna now prepares to impart even more profound and intimate wisdom to Arjuna. He prefaces this teaching by calling it *Raja Vidya Raja Guhyam* – the king of all knowledge, and the most confidential of all secrets. This knowledge is not merely theoretical; it is directly realizable, joyful to practice, and leads to the ultimate perfection.

Why "royal"? Because it illuminates the grandest truths concerning the Supreme King (the Lord Himself), His creation, and our eternal relationship with Him. It is comprehensive, deeply purifying, and offers the most direct path to understanding the essence of reality. Why "secret" or "confidential"? Not because it's meant to be arbitrarily hidden, but because its profound truths can only be grasped by those who approach it with faith (*Shraddha*), a non-envious heart, and a sincere desire to understand – qualities that open the door to deeper spiritual perception. This chapter is an invitation to unlock these profound secrets and tap into our innate spiritual potential.

The Royal Secret: Discover Gita's Most Profound Wisdom

Krishna begins to unveil the "Royal Secret" by explaining His own intricate relationship with the cosmos and all living beings. This is not abstract philosophy but a revelation of His all-pervading yet transcendent nature:

1. **All-Pervading Presence:** Krishna declares, "By Me, in My unmanifested form, this entire universe is pervaded. All beings are in Me, but I am not in them." (BG 9.4, paraphrased). This highlights His immanence – His divine energy permeates and sustains every atom of creation. Everything we see and experience rests within Him.

2. **Transcendental Detachment:** Simultaneously, while all beings rest in Him, He is not limited or affected by them or their actions, nor by the workings of the material world. He remains transcendent, the unattached sustainer and witness. This seemingly paradoxical nature – being intimately involved yet utterly free – is a hallmark of the Supreme.

3. **The Power of Maya (Divine Illusion):** Krishna explains that those whose minds are bewildered by His illusory energy (*Maya*) cannot perceive His true, imperishable, and supreme nature. They mistake Him for an ordinary being or are preoccupied with lesser, temporary pursuits. Maya creates the illusion of separateness and makes the material world seem all-important.

4. **The Path Beyond Illusion:** However, for the *Mahatmas* – the great souls who have taken shelter of His divine nature – this illusion is lifted. They understand Him as the inexhaustible origin of all beings and engage in His loving devotional service (Bhakti) with unwavering minds.

This "Royal Secret" reveals the Supreme Lord as the ultimate source, sustainer, and controller of everything, yet He remains ever accessible to those who approach Him with a pure heart and sincere devotion. Understanding this complex, intimate yet transcendental relationship is key to unlocking our spiritual potential. It shifts our perspective from seeing ourselves as isolated individuals in a random universe to recognizing our place within a divinely orchestrated, purposeful existence.

Learning from Visionaries: Insights from Mystics & Modern Leaders (Indian Context Where Possible)

The profound truths of Raja Vidya Raja Guhya Yoga, particularly the direct experience of the divine presence and an intimate loving relationship with the Supreme, have been echoed by mystics, saints, and spiritual visionaries across ages and traditions. Their lives and teachings often reflect a lived understanding of this "Kingly Secret."

- **Bhakti Saints of India:** Figures like Mirabai, Kabir, Tukaram, Surdas, and Chaitanya Mahaprabhu, from various parts of India, exemplified lives steeped in passionate devotion and an intuitive understanding of the Lord's pervasive presence and His loving nature.

Their songs and poems often express a deep, personal relationship with the Divine, transcending mere ritual and dogma, reflecting the essence of the devotional path Krishna highlights in this chapter. They demonstrated how the "Royal Secret" could be accessed through simple, heartfelt love and remembrance.

- **Sri Ramakrishna Paramahamsa & Ramana Maharshi:** These more recent sages from India, though following different spiritual paths (Ramakrishna embraced multiple paths including devotion, while Ramana Maharshi emphasized self-inquiry), both spoke of profound, direct experiences of the ultimate reality. Their teachings often guide seekers towards an inner realization that goes beyond intellectual understanding, resonating with the experiential nature of *Vigyana* linked to Raja Vidya.

- **Modern Leaders with Deep Purpose (Conceptual):** Even in contemporary life, leaders who operate from a place of profound integrity, a deep sense of interconnectedness, and an unwavering commitment to a purpose larger than themselves often exhibit an intuitive grasp of higher principles. While they may not use spiritual terminology, their actions might reflect a certain "inner knowing" or alignment with a universal ethical framework, hinting at the practical manifestation of a life lived with awareness of deeper truths.

These visionaries, through their lives and experiences, illustrate that the "Royal Secret" of the Gita is not confined to ancient scriptures but is a living, accessible truth for those who earnestly seek it and cultivate the necessary inner qualities.

Accessing Inner Knowing: Practical Steps for Tapping into Deep Intuition and Transformative Knowledge

Krishna doesn't just state these profound truths; He also reveals the most direct and joyful way to access this "Royal Knowledge" and the inner knowing it bestows. The key He emphasizes repeatedly in this chapter is **Bhakti – pure, loving devotional service.**

1. **The Power of Simple Devotion:** Krishna declares that He accepts even the simplest offerings – "If one offers Me with love and devotion a leaf, a flower, a fruit, or water, I will accept it." (BG 9.26). This is a radical statement. It means access to the Supreme is not dependent on elaborate rituals, vast wealth, or profound scholarship, but on the sincerity of one's love and devotion. This makes the path universally accessible.

2. **Cultivating Faith (Shraddha):** As mentioned earlier, this knowledge is revealed to those who have faith. This isn't blind belief, but an open, trusting heart willing to engage with the teachings and explore their truth. Faith creates the receptivity needed for this subtle wisdom to take root.

3. **Overcoming Envy and Cynicism:** Krishna specifically states this knowledge is for the non-envious (*anasuyave*). Envy, cynicism, and a fault-finding mentality create barriers to understanding spiritual truths. An open, appreciative, and humble attitude is essential.

4. **Purification of Heart and Mind:** Consistent engagement in spiritual practices like Karma Yoga (selfless action), Dhyana Yoga (meditation), and particularly acts of devotion, helps purify the mind of disturbances like greed, anger, and ego. A purer mind is like a clearer mirror, better able to reflect the subtle spiritual realities.

5. **Constant Remembrance and Glorification (Shravanam, Kirtanam, Smaranam):** Engaging in hearing about Lord's glories, chanting His name & remembering Him consistently keeps the mind focused on the Divine & gradually reveals His nature.

6. **Offering All Actions:** Krishna advises, "Whatever you do, whatever you eat, whatever you offer or give away, and whatever austerities you perform – do that as an offering unto Me." (BG 9.27). This transforms every aspect of life into an act of devotion and connection.

By sincerely engaging in these practices, especially those centered around loving devotion, the "Royal Secret" ceases to be a secret and becomes a lived experience, unlocking profound intuition and transformative inner knowing.

Chapter 9 Takeaway: The Joyful Path to Supreme Secret

Raja Vidya Raja Guhyam, the kingly and most confidential knowledge, reveals the Supreme Lord's pervasive yet transcendental nature and His intimate relationship with all beings. It is profound yet simple to access, not through complex austerities alone, but through the path of loving devotion (Bhakti). This knowledge is supremely purifying and, when realized, leads to direct experience of the Divine, liberating us from the cycle of birth and death and connecting us with our deepest spiritual potential. By understanding that the Lord accepts even the simplest offering made with love, and by dedicating our actions and our hearts to Him, we can transform our lives into a joyful journey of spiritual awakening and empowerment.

पत्रं पुष्पं फलं तोयं यो मे भक्त्या प्रयच्छति । तदहं भक्त्युपहृतमश्नामि प्रयतात्मनः ॥ ९.२६ ॥

Patraṁ puṣpaṁ phalaṁ toyaṁ yo me bhaktyā prayacchati | Tadahaṁ bhaktyupahṛitam-aśnāmi prayatātmanaḥ || 9.26 ||

Hindi: "जो कोई भक्त मेरे लिये प्रेम से पत्र, पुष्प, फल, जल आदि अर्पण करता है, उस शुद्ध मन वाले भक्त का वह प्रेमपूर्वक अर्पण किया हुआ मैं स्वीकार करता हूँ।"

English: "If one offers Me with love and devotion a leaf, a flower, a fruit, or water, I will accept it." ***(This verse beautifully expresses the simplicity and accessibility of the path of devotion.)***

Exercise: Practices for Personal Empowerment and Fostering Inner Growth

These practices are designed to help you connect with the "Royal Secret" and cultivate the inner qualities that unlock your spiritual potential.

1. **Practice: The Simple Offering of Devotion:**

Intention: Choose one day this week. Throughout that day, consciously practice the spirit of BG 9.27: "Whatever you do, whatever you eat, whatever you offer or give away... do that as an offering unto Me (the Supreme/Divine/Your Highest Ideal)."

Action: This doesn't require external ritual. It's internal shift.

- Before eating, silently offer your food with gratitude.
- As you work, mentally offer your efforts and skills.
- If you give charity or help someone, do it as an offering without expecting personal recognition.

Reflection: At the end of the day, journal for a few minutes: How did this practice of constant offering affect your attitude, your actions & state of mind? Did it bring a sense of greater purpose or connection to your daily activities?

2. **Practice: Contemplating Interconnectedness & Divine Pervasiveness:**

Contemplation: Spend 10-15 mins in a quiet space. Reflect on Krishna's statement that He pervades the entire universe in His unmanifest form & that all beings rest in Him.

Observation: Look at the natural world around you (a tree, the sky, an animal) or think about the people in your life. Try to gently sense or imagine an underlying unity, a divine energy or presence that connects and sustains everything.

Affirmation (Optional): You might silently repeat an affirmation like, "The Divine is present in all things," or "All beings rest in the One Supreme."

Journal: What feelings or insights arise as you contemplate this interconnectedness? How might recognizing this pervasive divine presence change how you interact with the world and others?

3. **Reflection Practice: Cultivating a Receptive Heart:**

Krishna states this "Royal Knowledge" is for the non-envious and faithful. Honestly reflect:

- "Are there any tendencies towards envy, cynicism, or excessive skepticism in my own thinking that might create a barrier to understanding or experiencing deeper spiritual truths?"
- "What small steps can I take to cultivate a more open, trusting & appreciative heart non-enviousness) in my approach to spiritual learning and life in general?"

Journal your thoughts for cultivating these qualities.

(These practices, centered on devotion, contemplation, and heart-centered qualities, help you to personally access the transformative power of the "Royal Secret" shared in this chapter, leading to inner growth and empowerment.)

Adhyay 10: See the Spark Everywhere – Find Wonder in the Ordinary

(Vibhuti Yoga – The Yoga of Divine Glories)

From Profound Truth to Palpable Presence: Arjuna's Eagerness

In Adhyay 9, Lord Krishna revealed the "Royal Knowledge" and "Most Confidential Secret" – His all-pervading yet transcendent nature, and the simple yet profound path of loving devotion (Bhakti) as the key to accessing Him. Having heard these supreme truths, Arjuna is filled with awe and a deep desire to understand more. His delusion is vanishing, and he now accepts Krishna as the Supreme Personality of Godhead, the source of all existence. Eager to deepen his connection and perception, Arjuna requests Krishna to describe in more detail His divine opulences (*Vibhutis*) – those specific manifestations through which He pervades all the worlds. Arjuna wishes to learn how to think of Krishna constantly and in what various forms He can be meditated upon.

Krishna lovingly agrees, explaining that His glories are indeed infinite, but He will describe some of His principal manifestations. This unveiling is the essence of *Vibhuti Yoga*. It's a practical path that helps us train our minds and hearts to perceive the divine spark not just in a remote heaven or abstract concept, but right here, in the vibrant tapestry of creation, in the excellent, the powerful, and the beautiful aspects of our everyday world. It's about transforming ordinary sight into sacred vision.

Awaken Your Eyes: Perceive the Divine in Daily Life

The concept of *Vibhuti* refers to divine glories, specific opulences, extraordinary powers, or prominent manifestations that particularly reveal the presence, majesty, and magnificence of the Supreme Lord. Krishna begins by establishing Himself as the ultimate source of everything: "I am the origin of all gods and great sages... I am the Self, O Gudakesha (Arjuna), seated in the hearts of all creatures. I am the beginning, the middle, and the end of all beings." (BG 10.2, 10.20, paraphrased).

Then, He proceeds to list a dazzling array of His prominent Vibhutis, encouraging us to see Him in:

Cosmic & Natural Wonders: Among Adityas, He is Vishnu; among lights, the radiant sun; among stars, the moon. He is the Himalayas among mountains, the ocean among bodies of water, the sacred Ganga river. He is the life-giving wind, the all-consuming fire, and even death itself.

Divine Beings & Scriptural Elements: He is Indra among the demigods, Shiva among the Rudras, Kubera (lord of wealth) among Yakshas and Rakshasas. He is the Sama Veda among the Vedas, the Gayatri among poetic meters, the sacred syllable Om (ॐ) among all sounds.

Qualities & Inner Principles: He is consciousness in living beings, the mind among the senses, intelligence among the intelligent, glory among the glorious, determination, forgiveness, and truthfulness.

Excellence in All Forms: Among priests, He is Brihaspati; among generals, Kartikeya; among sages, Narada and Vyasa. He is the lion among beasts, Garuda (Vishnu's eagle carrier) among birds, the wish-fulfilling Kamadhenu cow, the mighty Banyan tree among trees. Among warriors and heroes, He even identifies Himself with Arjuna among the Pandavas, highlighting Arjuna's own divine potential. He is Vasudeva (His own father) among the Vrishnis.

This extensive, though not exhaustive, list serves a profound purpose. It trains us to look for the divine signature in everything that is powerful, beautiful, excellent, profound, or essential for life. Krishna's message is clear: wherever you perceive extraordinary brilliance, strength, beauty, intelligence, or any form of supreme excellence, know that it is but a spark, a tiny fragment, of His infinite splendor. This practice gradually expands our awareness, helping us to see the sacred not just in temples or during prayer, but in the everyday world – in nature, in art, in human talent, and within ourselves.

Stories That Inspire: How Awe Transformed Lives (India & Beyond)

The recognition of divine magnificence, the experience of awe in the face of something extraordinarily beautiful or powerful, has often been a transformative catalyst in people's lives. These moments can shift our perspective, fill us with humility, and ignite a deeper sense of connection and purpose.

- **A Scientist's Humility:** Imagine a dedicated astronomer gazing through a powerful telescope, witnessing the birth of stars in a distant nebula or the unfathomable scale of galaxies. While their work is scientific, the sheer grandeur and intricate order of the cosmos can evoke a profound sense of awe, a feeling that transcends mere data. This experience can lead to a deep humility and an appreciation for an intelligence or power far beyond human comprehension – a personal glimpse of a cosmic Vibhuti.

- **An Artist's Inspiration:** Many artists, musicians, and poets throughout history have described their greatest works as flowing *through* them from an inspired source, often triggered by the beauty of nature, a profound human emotion, or a spiritual insight. The majestic snow-capped peaks of the Himalayas (a Vibhuti mentioned by Krishna) have inspired countless seekers and artists, awakening a sense of the sublime and the eternal. This creative flow, born from awe, can feel like a direct connection to a divine wellspring.

- **A Devotee's Heartfelt Connection:** In India, many devotees experience the Divine through specific forms or deities, each considered a manifestation of the Supreme. Seeing the vibrant rituals, hearing the soul-stirring bhajans, or feeling the collective energy in a sacred place can evoke intense emotions of love, joy, and surrender. A devotee seeing the majestic form of Lord Jagannath during Rath Yatra in Puri, or feeling the serene presence in a quiet temple, might experience a profound connection, recognizing a specific Vibhuti that speaks directly to their heart, transforming their inner state.

These experiences, whether in nature, art, science, or spiritual practice, are moments where the veil thins, and we glimpse the extraordinary within or behind the ordinary. Such moments of awe and connection, fueled by recognizing divine sparks, can reorient our lives, filling them with renewed meaning and gratitude.

The Gratitude Effect: Cultivate Deep Appreciation & Reverence

The practice of Vibhuti Yoga – consciously looking for and acknowledging the divine glories in the world – naturally cultivates a profound sense of gratitude and reverence. When we stop taking the wonders around us for granted and begin to see them as manifestations of a higher intelligence, power, or love, our hearts naturally respond with appreciation.

- **From Entitlement to Appreciation:** Often, we move through life with a sense of entitlement or a focus on what's lacking. Vibhuti Yoga shifts this perspective. The taste of fresh water, the warmth of the sun, the beauty of a flower, the intelligence of a child, the kindness of a stranger – when seen as sparks of the Divine, they cease to be ordinary and become gifts to be cherished.

- **The Power of Gratitude:** Modern psychology has extensively documented the benefits of gratitude. Regularly practicing gratitude is linked to increased happiness, reduced stress and depression, improved physical health, better sleep, and stronger relationships. By recognizing the divine opulences, we find endless reasons to be grateful.

- **Cultivating Reverence:** Reverence is a deeper form of respect and awe, an acknowledgment of something sacred and greater than ourselves. Perceiving the Vibhutis fosters reverence for life, for nature, for the intricate order of the cosmos, and for the divine source of all. This attitude of reverence protects us from arrogance and cynicism, opening our hearts to humility and wonder.

Practical Ways to Cultivate Gratitude and Reverence:

- **Keep a Gratitude Journal:** Daily list things you are thankful for, from the simple to the profound.

- **Express Thanks Consciously:** Make it a point to genuinely thank people, and also silently thank the source for the blessings in your life.

- **Spend Mindful Time in Nature:** Observe the beauty and complexity of nature with an attitude of appreciation and wonder.

- **Acknowledge Excellence:** When you witness skill, talent, or virtue in others, appreciate it as a divine spark.

By actively cultivating gratitude and reverence through the lens of Vibhuti Yoga, our experience of life becomes richer, more joyful, and deeply connected to the sacred.

Chapter 10 Takeaway: A World Saturated with Divinity

Vibhuti Yoga is a beautiful and accessible path that transforms our perception of the world. It teaches us that the Divine is not remote or abstract but vibrantly present in every aspect of creation, especially in its most excellent and glorious manifestations. By learning to "awaken our eyes" and see these divine sparks everywhere – in nature, in others, and within ourselves – we cultivate a continuous sense of wonder, deep gratitude, and a loving connection with the Supreme. This practice doesn't require us to retreat from the world but to engage with it more fully, seeing it as a magnificent display of divine artistry and power. It makes spirituality not a Sunday affair, but a 24/7 experience of living in a world saturated with divinity.

यद्यद्वभिूतमित्सत्त्वं श्रीमदूर्जतिमेव वा । तत्तदेवावगच्छ त्वं मम तेजोंऽशसम्भवम् ॥ १०.४१ ॥

Yad yad vibhūtimat sattvaṁ śrīmad ūrjitam eva vā | Tat tad evāvagaccha tvaṁ mama tejo-'ṁśa-sambhavam || 10.41 ||

Hindi: "जो भी ऐश्वर्ययुक्त, कान्तियुक्त और शक्तियुक्त वस्तु है, उस उसको तुम मेरे तेज के अंश से ही उत्पन्न हुआ जानो।"

English: "Know that all opulent, beautiful, and glorious creations spring from but a spark of My splendor." ***(This verse encapsulates the essence of Vibhuti Yoga – seeing all excellence as a manifestation of the Divine's glory.)***

Exercise: Find Daily Magic – Practices to Develop Wonder & Appreciation

These practices are designed to help you actively look for and appreciate the divine glories (Vibhutis) in your everyday life, fostering wonder and gratitude.

1. **Practice: "Vibhuti Spotting" – Your Daily Scan for Excellence:**

Intention: For one day (or a few days this week), make a conscious effort to identify 3-5 "Vibhutis" – moments, objects, beings, or qualities that exhibit extraordinary beauty, power, intelligence, skill, kindness, or any form of excellence. These don't have to be grand; they can be simple.

Examples: The intricate design of a spider's web, the vibrant colors of a sunset over the Mumbai skyline, the powerful rhythm of the ocean waves, the focused skill of an artisan at work, an act of unexpected generosity from a stranger, the brilliance of a new idea, the resilience of a plant growing in a difficult place.

Action: When you spot a Vibhuti, pause for a moment. Acknowledge its excellence. Silently (or in a journal), recognize it as a spark of the Divine, saying to yourself, "This too is a manifestation of that Supreme Splendor."

Reflection: How does consciously looking for these sparks change your perception of your day?

2. **Practice: Gratitude List Infused with Reverence:**

Routine: At the end of your day, list 3-5 specific things you are grateful for from that day.

Deepen with Reverence: For each item on your list, take an extra moment. Instead of just being glad it happened, try to see it as a manifestation of a greater intelligence, abundance, divine grace, or a specific Vibhuti. For example:

- Instead of "Grateful for a good meal," perhaps "Grateful for the incredible bounty of nature (a Vibhuti) that provided this nourishing food, and the skill (a Vibhuti) that prepared it."
- Instead of "Grateful for a helpful colleague," perhaps "Grateful for the spark of kindness and intelligence (Vibhutis) shown by my colleague."

Notice the Shift: Does this deeper reflection change the quality of your gratitude?

3. **Reflection Practice: Journey into Awe:**

Recall: Bring to mind a time in your life when you felt a profound sense of awe or wonder. This could have been in nature (like witnessing a majestic mountain range or a starry night), listening to a breathtaking piece of music, seeing an extraordinary work of art, witnessing an act of incredible courage or compassion, or even a moment of deep scientific insight.

Describe & Feel: Try to relive that experience in your mind. What did you see, hear, feel? What was the emotional impact?

Connect: How might that experience have been a direct encounter with a Vibhuti, a powerful manifestation of divine glory, beauty, or power? How did that moment affect your perspective on life, even if temporarily? Journal your reflections.

(By consciously seeking and appreciating these divine sparks, you transform the mundane into the magical, filling your life with wonder, gratitude, and a tangible sense of connection to the all-pervading Divine.)

Adhyay 11: The Cosmic View – Embracing Our Universal Connection

(Visvarupa Darshana Yoga – The Yoga of the Vision of the Cosmic Form)

From Hearing to Seeing: Arjuna's Deep Desire

In Adhyay 10, Lord Krishna revealed His divine opulences (*Vibhutis*), explaining how He is the source and essence of all that is excellent and magnificent in creation. Hearing these glories, Arjuna's delusion has been dispelled. He accepts Krishna unequivocally as the Supreme Personality of Godhead, the ultimate origin and sustainer of all beings. His faith and understanding have deepened. Yet, a profound desire now arises within him: to move from *hearing* about Krishna's cosmic majesty to directly *seeing* His Universal Form (*Visvarupa*) – that all-encompassing divine form in which the entire universe is contained.

Filled with devotion and humility, Arjuna makes his plea: "O Supreme Lord, You are as You have declared Yourself to be. Nevertheless, I desire to see Your divine, cosmic form, if You think I am capable of seeing it." (BG 11.3-4, paraphrased). This request marks the beginning of one of the most awe-inspiring and transformative revelations in the Bhagavad Gita: the Visvarupa Darshana Yoga, the yoga of beholding the Lord's Cosmic Form. It is a chapter that expands our awareness to embrace the profound interconnectedness and ultimate unity of all existence within the Divine.

Expanding Your Awareness: The Revelation of the Visvarupa

Understanding Arjuna's sincere desire, Lord Krishna, out of His causeless mercy, agrees to reveal His Universal Form. He states, however, that Arjuna cannot perceive this transcendental form with his present material eyes. Therefore, Krishna bestows upon him *divya-chakshu* – divine vision – enabling him to witness the unimaginable.

What Arjuna then beholds is beyond human comprehension, a spectacle of infinite majesty, terror, and wonder, all at once:

- **Infinite Forms, Infinite Splendor:** He sees countless forms, countless mouths, eyes, arms, and bellies, extending in all directions without beginning, middle, or end. The form is adorned with divine ornaments and celestial weapons, radiating an effulgence like that of thousands of suns rising simultaneously in the sky.

- **The Universe Within:** Within that single Cosmic Form, Arjuna sees the entire universe with all its diverse manifestations – all demigods, sages, celestial beings, planets, stars, and every living creature – all contained and moving within Krishna's transcendental body.

- **Time, the Destroyer (Kala-Rupa):** A particularly terrifying aspect of this vision is Krishna revealing His form as Time (*Kala*), the all-devouring destroyer of worlds. Arjuna sees the warriors on both sides of the Kurukshetra battlefield – including Bhishma, Drona, Karna, and even his own brothers – rushing into Krishna's fiery mouths, being crushed between His terrible teeth. Krishna explains that these warriors are already slain by His arrangement (as Time), and Arjuna is merely to be an instrument in their physical demise.

- **Arjuna's Overwhelmed Reaction:** Witnessing this unfathomable form, Arjuna is struck with overwhelming awe, fear, and astonishment. His hair stands on end, he bows his head, and with folded hands, he begins to offer prayers, glorifying Krishna's limitless power and seeking forgiveness for any past acts of familiarity where he might have addressed Krishna as a mere friend, unaware of His supreme majesty. He is utterly humbled and shaken.

This divine vision shatters Arjuna's limited human perspective. It directly demonstrates the absolute omnipotence of the Divine, the ultimate interconnectedness of all beings and events, the relentless march of time, and the truth that everything, from creation to destruction, emanates from and rests within the Supreme Lord. Eventually, trembling and overwhelmed, Arjuna pleads with Krishna to withdraw this terrifying cosmic manifestation and return to His gentle, familiar four-armed form (as Lord Vishnu) or His two-armed human-like form.

Seeing the Big Picture: Learning from Historical and Modern Examples of Grasping Universal Unity

While Arjuna's direct vision of the Visvarupa is a unique divine revelation, the human yearning to grasp the "big picture" and experience a sense of universal unity or cosmic consciousness is a recurring theme across cultures and throughout history.

- **Mystical Experiences:** Mystics and sages from various traditions (Hindu yogis, Sufi saints, Christian mystics, Buddhist masters) have often described profound experiences of oneness, where the illusion of separateness dissolves, and they perceive an underlying unity or interconnectedness with all of existence. These experiences, often achieved through deep meditation, prayer, or spiritual discipline, echo the essence of what the Visvarupa reveals – a reality far beyond our everyday limited perception.
- **The "Overview Effect" in Astronauts:** Modern astronauts who have viewed Earth from space often report a profound cognitive shift known as the "Overview Effect." Seeing our planet as a tiny, fragile blue marble suspended in the vastness of space, without visible borders, can evoke an overwhelming sense of interconnectedness, global unity, and a deep responsibility for the planet and all its inhabitants. It's a modern parallel to "seeing the big picture" that can be life-altering.

- **Insights from Deep Ecology and Systems Thinking:** Scientific fields like deep ecology and systems theory emphasize the intricate interdependence of all elements within an ecosystem or a complex system. They demonstrate how the health and behavior of one part affect all other parts, highlighting a fundamental interconnectedness that mirrors the cosmic unity seen in the Visvarupa. No being or event exists in true isolation.
- **Spontaneous Moments of Unity:** Sometimes, individuals report spontaneous moments of profound insight or oneness, perhaps during times of intense crisis, deep connection with nature (e.g., gazing at a star-filled sky or the vast ocean), or through experiences with art or music that evoke a sense of transcendence. These glimpses, however fleeting, can leave a lasting impression of a reality beyond the mundane.

These examples, though different in nature from Arjuna's direct divine vision, suggest that the human mind and heart are capable of, and often yearn for, experiences that expand awareness beyond the limited self and connect with a larger, universal reality.

Inner Vision Techniques: Methods for Meditative Visualization & Cultivating Cosmic Awareness

While we cannot demand to see the Visvarupa as Arjuna did, we can employ practices that help cultivate a sense of cosmic awareness, interconnectedness, and a glimpse of the "bigger picture." These techniques aim to expand our inner vision and reduce the dominance of the ego's narrow perspective:

1. **Meditative Visualization for Expanding Awareness:**

The Expanding Circle: Sit quietly and begin by becoming aware of your physical body. Then, gradually expand your awareness outwards: to the room you are in, the building, your neighborhood, your city (e.g., Mumbai), your country (India), the continent, the planet Earth. Continue expanding your awareness to include the solar system, the Milky Way galaxy, and finally, the vast, immeasurable cosmos filled with countless galaxies. Feel your connection to this immense whole. Then, gently bring your awareness back, stage by stage, to your physical body, carrying that sense of expanded connection.

Visualizing Light & Energy: Imagine yourself as a point of light or energy. Then visualize all other living beings also as points of light. See these lights interconnected, forming a vast network or field of consciousness, all originating from and returning to a single, brilliant source of light representing the Divine.

2. **Contemplation on Interdependence (Pratītyasamutpāda thinking):**

Choose an everyday object (e.g., your food, your clothing, your phone). Spend some time reflecting on all the interconnected elements and processes that brought this object to you: the natural resources, the sunlight, the water, the plants or animals, the countless people involved in growing, harvesting, manufacturing, transporting, and selling. Recognizing this deep web of interdependence helps dissolve the illusion of separateness.

3. **Practicing Awe (Extending Vibhuti Yoga):**

Actively seek out experiences that naturally evoke awe: spend time in grand natural settings, listen to powerful music, view inspiring art, read about scientific discoveries that reveal the complexity and beauty of the universe. Use these moments not just for enjoyment, but as opportunities to contemplate the vastness, intelligence, and unity underlying existence.

4. **Mantras and Affirmations for Unity:**

Silently repeat mantras that emphasize oneness, such as "Soham" (I am That) or "Aham Brahmasmi" (I am Brahman), understanding "Brahman" as the reality.

Use affirmations like: "I am connected to all life," "Universe is within me & I am within the universe," "All is One."

These practices, undertaken regularly, can help shift our default perspective from a narrow, ego-centric view to a more expansive, interconnected, and cosmic awareness.

Chapter 11 Takeaway: Embracing the Awe of Universal Connection

The vision of the Universal Form (Visvarupa Darshana) granted to Arjuna is one of the most profound and awe-inspiring moments in spiritual literature. It offers a glimpse into the ultimate reality of the Divine's omnipresence, omnipotence, and the interconnectedness of all existence within that Supreme Being. While such direct, divine revelation is exceedingly rare, the experience underscores the transformative power of expanding our awareness beyond the limited self. By cultivating practices that foster a sense of cosmic awareness, interconnectedness, and awe, we can begin to loosen the grip of the ego, reduce feelings of isolation, and develop a deeper compassion for all beings. Embracing this "big picture" perspective helps us navigate life with greater wisdom, humility, and a profound sense of our place within the magnificent, unified whole.

तत्रैकस्थं जगत्कृत्स्नं प्रविभक्तमनेकधा । अपश्यद्देवदेवस्य शरीरे पाण्डवस्तदा ॥ ११.१३ ॥

Tatraikasthaṁ jagat-kṛitsnaṁ pravibhaktam-anekadhā |

Apaśyad-devadevasya śarīre pāṇḍavas-tadā || 11.13 ||

Hindi: "उस समय पाण्डुपुत्र अर्जुन ने उन देवों के देव (श्रीकृष्ण) के शरीर में अनेक प्रकार से विभक्त सम्पूर्ण जगत् को एक स्थान पर स्थित देखा।"

English: "At that time Arjuna could see in the universal form of the Lord the unlimited expansions of the universe situated in one place although divided into many, many thousands." ***(This verse describes Arjuna***

witnessing the entire universe, with its manifold divisions, congregated in one place within Krishna's Cosmic Form.)

Exercise: Practices to Grasp and Feel Universal Unity

These exercises are designed to help you cultivate a felt sense of interconnectedness and expand your awareness towards a more universal perspective.

1. **Practice: Expanding Circle of Awareness Visualization (10-15 minutes):**

Preparation: Sit comfortably in a quiet space, close your eyes, and take a few calming breaths.

Starting Point: Bring your awareness to your physical body, noticing its sensations.

Gradual Expansion:

- Imagine your awareness gently expanding to fill the room you are in.
- Then, let it expand further to encompass the entire building... your neighborhood... your city (e.g., the vastness of Mumbai).
- Continue expanding to your state (Maharashtra)... your country (India)... the continent... the entire planet Earth, seeing it suspended in space.
- Expand further to include the moon, the sun, our solar system... our Milky Way galaxy... and then countless other galaxies, filling the vast expanse of the cosmos.

Feeling Oneness: As your awareness expands, try to feel a sense of connection with everything it encompasses. Rest in this feeling of vastness and interconnectedness for a few moments.

Gentle Return: Slowly, gently, bring your awareness back, stage by stage – from the cosmos to your galaxy, solar system, planet, country, city, room, and finally back to your physical body. Carry that expansive feeling with you.

2. **Practice: Web of Interdependence Reflection (10-15 minutes):**

Choose an Object: Select a simple, everyday object near you – perhaps your morning cup of tea/coffee, a piece of fruit, an item of clothing, or your smartphone.

Trace its Origins: Spend 10-15 minutes mentally (or by journaling) tracing back all the elements, processes, and people involved in bringing that object to you.

For example, for a cup of tea: Consider the tea leaves (grown by farmers, perhaps far away, needing sun, rain, soil), the water (sourced, purified, transported), the sugar or milk (if any, and their own complex origins), the cup (made from clay or other materials, crafted, fired, transported), the electricity or gas that heated the water, the people involved in packaging, shipping, selling.

Reflect on Interconnection: As you uncover this vast web of connections, reflect on how deeply interdependent your life is with countless other beings, natural resources, and processes across the globe. How does this make you feel?

3. **Reflection Practice: Moments of Awe and Unity:**

Recall: Think of a specific time in your life when you felt a profound sense of awe, wonder, or a feeling of being deeply connected to something much larger than yourself (e.g., witnessing a spectacular natural phenomenon, a deeply moving artistic performance, a moment of intense human connection or compassion, a spiritual experience).

Journal: Describe the experience in as much detail as you can remember. What triggered it? What were your thoughts and feelings? How did this experience impact your perspective on yourself, others, or life in general, even if only for a short time? How can you consciously create more opportunities in your life to invite such "big picture" moments or feelings of awe and unity?

(Cultivating a sense of universal connection and grasping the "big picture" is an ongoing practice. These exercises help to gently stretch the boundaries of our awareness, fostering humility, compassion, and a deeper appreciation for the magnificent, interconnected tapestry of existence.)

Adhyay 12: Lead with Heart – Find Strength in Purpose & Devotion

(Bhakti Yoga – The Yoga of Devotion)

The Path of the Heart: Arjuna Seeks Clarity

After the breathtaking revelation of the Universal Form (Visvarupa) in Adhyay 11, which showcased Lord Krishna's infinite, all-encompassing, and sometimes terrifying cosmic majesty, Arjuna is filled with awe but also seeks practical clarity on the path of worship. He now asks a pivotal question: Who is considered more perfect in yoga? Is it those who are constantly devoted to Krishna's personal, manifest form, worshipping Him with unwavering faith? Or is it those who worship the impersonal, unmanifest, imperishable Absolute (Akshara Brahman), which was discussed in earlier chapters?

This question is crucial for seekers trying to navigate their spiritual path. It addresses the difference between approaching the Divine through a personal, relational framework versus an impersonal, abstract one. Krishna's answer in this chapter forms the essence of *Bhakti Yoga*, the yoga of devotion, revealing it as a direct, accessible, and deeply rewarding path to connect with the Supreme, a path that truly leads with the heart.

Unconditional Love & Surrender: Exploring the Transformative Power of Devotion

Lord Krishna responds to Arjuna with clear and emphatic guidance:

The Preeminence of Personal Devotion: He declares that those who fix their minds on His personal form, always engaged in His worship with supreme, steadfast faith, are considered by Him to be most perfect in yoga. This path involves a direct, loving relationship with the Divine, perceived as the Supreme Person.

The Path of the Unmanifest – Acknowledged but Arduous: Krishna acknowledges that those who worship the unmanifest, imperishable, all-pervading, inconceivable, unchanging, immovable, and constant Absolute (Brahman) – restraining all their senses, being equally disposed to everyone, and engaged in the welfare of all beings – also ultimately reach Him. However, He points out that for embodied beings (those who identify with the physical body), the path of realizing the unmanifest Absolute is exceedingly difficult (*kleśo 'dhikataras teṣām*). Progress is more arduous because identifying with something that has no form or tangible attributes is challenging for the mind, which is accustomed to dealing with forms and concepts.

The Ease and Directness of Bhakti Yoga: In contrast, Bhakti Yoga, the path of loving devotion, is often more natural and joyful for most people. It allows for a personal, reciprocal relationship with the Divine, engaging the emotions, mind, and senses in service and remembrance. Key elements that make Bhakti Yoga so powerful and transformative include:

- **Shraddha (Faith):** An unwavering, loving faith in the Supreme Lord as a person, as our ultimate well-wisher and protector.
- **Prema (Divine Love):** Cultivating pure, selfless, and unconditional love for God. This love becomes the driving force for all actions and thoughts.
- **Smaranam (Constant Remembrance):** Keeping the Lord constantly in one's mind – His names, forms, qualities, pastimes, and teachings.
- **Kirtanam (Glorification):** Singing or chanting the Lord's names and glories, individually or congregationally.
- **Seva (Loving Service):** Performing all actions, including one's daily duties, as a loving service to the Supreme. This transforms work into worship.
- **Sharanagati (Complete Surrender):** Taking complete refuge in the Lord, trusting in His protection and guidance, and aligning one's will with His. Krishna makes a profound promise to those who practice this surrender: *"For those who worship Me, giving up all their activities unto Me and being devoted to Me without deviation, engaged in devotional service and always meditating upon Me, having fixed their minds upon Me, O son of Pṛthā – for them I am the swift deliverer from the ocean of birth and death."* (BG 12.6-7).

This path of love and surrender purifies the heart, dissolves the ego, alleviates anxieties, and creates an unbreakable, joyful bond with the Divine, leading directly to peace, fulfillment, and liberation.

Lessons from Devotion: Drawing Inspiration from Historical Figures

Throughout history, many souls have walked the path of Bhakti, their lives radiating the transformative power of divine love and inspiring countless others.

- **Mirabai (India, 16th Century):** A Rajput princess and poet-saint, Mirabai's life was a testament to unwavering, ecstatic devotion to Lord Krishna. Despite facing severe opposition, persecution, and attempts on her life from her own family for her all-consuming love for Krishna (whom she considered her true husband), she never wavered. Her soul-stirring bhajans (devotional songs) express the deepest pangs of separation and the highest joys of union with her beloved Lord, inspiring millions even today with the power of pure, fearless devotion.

- **Rumi (Persia, 13th Century):** Jalāl ad-Dīn Muhammad Rūmī, the Sufi mystic and poet, expressed the soul's intense longing for the Divine Beloved through some of the world's most beautiful and profound poetry. His teachings emphasize love as the core of spiritual experience, the "alchemy" that transforms the base metal of the ego into the gold of divine consciousness. His work highlights the universal nature of the heart's yearning for connection with the Supreme.

- **Mother Teresa (Modern Example of Devotion through Service):** While rooted in the Christian tradition, Mother Teresa's life of extraordinary selfless service to the poorest of the poor, the sick, and the dying in Kolkata was fueled by her deep love for God, whom she saw in every individual she served. Her relentless work, undertaken with profound compassion and often in the face of immense hardship, can be seen as a powerful expression of *seva* (service) driven by *bhakti* (devotion), demonstrating how divine love can translate into impactful action for the welfare of all.

These figures, and countless others, demonstrate that the path of devotion is not about mere sentimentality, but about a profound reorientation of one's entire being towards the Divine, leading to extraordinary strength, compassion, and inner transformation.

Devotion in Daily Life: Cultivating a Devotional Mindset Towards Your Purpose and Actions

Bhakti Yoga isn't confined to temples, mosques, churches, or formal rituals; it is an attitude, a heartfelt connection that can and should permeate every aspect of our daily lives. Here's how to cultivate a devotional mindset:

1. **See the Divine in All Beings:** Strive to recognize the spark of the Divine (Atman) within every living

entity. This understanding naturally fosters respect, kindness, and compassion in your interactions with others, transforming relationships.

2. **Offer Your Work (Bhakti-Infused Karma Yoga):** As Krishna advised in Adhyay 9, perform your daily duties and professional work not just for personal gain or obligation, but as a dedicated offering to the Supreme (or your highest ideal/purpose). Dedicate your skills, efforts, and intentions, transforming work into a form of worship.

3. **Cultivate Continuous Gratitude:** Maintain an attitude of gratitude for all blessings, big and small – your life, health, relationships, opportunities, even challenges (for the lessons they bring). See these not as random occurrences but as expressions of a benevolent higher intelligence or divine grace.

4. **Simple Acts of Remembrance & Connection:** Integrate small, conscious acts of remembrance throughout your day. This could be a silent prayer before meals, a moment of gratitude upon waking, mentally chanting a divine name while commuting or doing chores, or simply pausing to appreciate a moment of beauty and connect it to its source.

5. **Find Your Personal Connection:** The Divine can be approached in many forms and through many moods. Explore what form, name, quality, or aspect of God (or a universal loving presence) most deeply

resonates with your heart. A personal connection makes devotion more intimate and joyful.

6. **Associate with Like-Minded Seekers (Satsanga):** Spending time with others who are also on a spiritual path, sharing insights, and engaging in devotional practices together can provide immense support, inspiration, and encouragement.

By weaving these simple practices into your daily rhythm, your life gradually becomes infused with a sense of sacredness, purpose, and loving connection.

The Qualities of a Devotee Dear to Krishna

Towards the end of Adhyay 12 (verses 13-20), Krishna lovingly describes the qualities of the devotee who is exceedingly dear to Him. These qualities are not prerequisites for starting on the path of devotion, but rather virtues that naturally blossom in one who sincerely practices Bhakti Yoga. Cultivating these qualities helps deepen our connection with the Divine:

- One who is not envious but is a kind friend to all living entities.
- Who does not think himself a proprietor and is free from false ego.
- Who is equal in both happiness and distress, tolerant, and always satisfied.

- Self-controlled, and engaged in devotional service with determination, his mind and intelligence fixed on Me.
- He by whom no one is put into difficulty and who is not disturbed by anyone.
- Who is equipoised in honor and dishonor, fear and anxiety.
- Who is independent of the ordinary course of activities, pure, expert, without unnecessary concern, free from all pains, and not striving for the results of his actions.
- Who is equal to friends and enemies, and who is equipoised in fame and infamy, heat and cold, happiness and distress.
- Who is free from all undesirable association, always silent (not engaging in frivolous talk), and satisfied with anything.
- Who has no residence (is not attached to any particular place), whose mind is fixed, and who is engaged in devotional service – such a person is very dear to Me.

These sublime qualities reflect a heart purified by love for the Divine, leading to harmony within oneself and with all of creation.

Chapter 12 Takeaway: The Swift Path of the Heart

Bhakti Yoga, the path of loving devotion and surrender, stands out as a direct, joyful, and powerful means to connect with the Supreme Lord and attain ultimate liberation. Krishna Himself extols this path as being most dear to Him and assures His devotees of His swift deliverance. It transforms our relationship with the Divine from an abstract concept or distant goal into a living, loving, and deeply personal reality. By cultivating faith, love, remembrance, service, and surrender, and by striving to embody the qualities of a true devotee, we open our hearts to experience the profound strength, peace, and bliss that come from an unbreakable connection with the source of all love.

ये तु सर्वाणि कर्माणि मयि संन्यस्य मत्पराः । अनन्येनैव योगेन मां ध्यायन्त उपासते ॥ १२.६ ॥

Ye tu sarvāṇi karmāṇi mayi sannyasya mat-parāḥ |
Ananyenaiva yogena māṁ dhyāyanta upāsate || 12.6 ||

तेषामहं समुद्धरता मृत्युसंसारसागरात् । भवामि नचिरात्पार्थ मय्यावेशितचेतसाम् ॥ १२.७ ॥

Teṣām ahaṁ samuddhartā mṛtyu-saṁsāra-sāgarāt | Bhavāmi na cirāt pārtha mayy-āveśita-cetasām || 12.7 ||

Hindi (12.6-7): "परन्तु जो मेरे परायण रहने वाले भक्तजन सम्पूर्ण कर्मों को मुझमें अर्पण करके अनन्य योग से मेरा ही ध्यान करते हुए मेरी उपासना करते हैं, हे पार्थ! उन मुझमें चित्त लगाने वालों का मैं शीघ्र ही मृत्युरूप संसार-समुद्र से उद्धार करने वाला होता हूँ।"

English (12.6-7): "But those who worship Me, giving up all their activities unto Me and being devoted to Me without deviation, engaged in devotional service and always meditating upon Me, having fixed their minds upon Me, O son of Pṛthā—for them I am the swift deliverer from the ocean of birth and death." ***(This pair of verses powerfully conveys Krishna's promise to His devoted worshipers.)***

Reflection Practices to Deepen Your Connection

These exercises aim to help you explore and cultivate a devotional connection in your life, whether to the Divine in a specific form or to your highest ideal or purpose.

Practice: Heart-Centered Meditation (10-15 minutes):

- **Settle & Connect:** Sit comfortably and bring your awareness to your heart center (the middle of your chest). Imagine a warm, radiant light glowing there.
- **Cultivate Feelings:** Gently try to cultivate feelings of love, gratitude, or peace within this heart space. You might think of someone you love deeply, a moment of profound beauty, or a quality of the Divine that inspires you (e.g., compassion, unconditional love, strength).
- **Offer or Connect:** If you have a chosen form of the Divine, a spiritual guide, or a sacred mantra, mentally offer these feelings of love and gratitude. Alternatively, you can radiate these positive feelings outwards, wishing well-being for all.
- **Rest in the Feeling:** Spend a few minutes simply resting in whatever positive emotions or sense of connection arises. Don't force anything; just be open.

Practice: Offering an Action with Devotion:

- **Choose an Action:** Select a simple, routine action you will perform today (e.g., preparing a meal, cleaning, helping someone, your commute).
- **Set a Devotional Intention:** Before you begin, take a moment to consciously offer this action with a feeling of love or service. You might offer it to your chosen form of the Divine, to a higher purpose, or for the well-being of all beings. For example: "May this action be an offering of love," or "May this effort serve a greater good."

- **Perform with Awareness:** As you do the action, try to maintain this feeling of offering and connection in your heart. Notice if this changes your experience of the task. Does it feel less like a chore and more like a meaningful act?

Reflection Practice: Cultivating Devotional Qualities:

- **Review:** Look back at the qualities of a devotee dear to Krishna (listed in the section above, from BG 12.13-20, such as being non-envious, kind, equal in happiness/distress, content, self-controlled).
- **Identify & Aspire:** Which one or two of these qualities do you feel most drawn to cultivate in your own life right now? Why?
- **Small Step:** What is one small, concrete step you can take this week to consciously practice and nurture that chosen quality in your interactions or inner attitude? Journal your thoughts and commitment.

Reflection Practice: Your Personal Connection:

- **Resonance:** What form, name, image, or concept of the Divine (or a universal loving intelligence, or your highest guiding principle) most deeply resonates with your heart and mind? It could be a traditional deity, a quality like 'Love' or 'Truth', a spiritual figure, or nature itself.
- **Cultivating Connection:** How can you create more opportunities in your daily life to consciously connect with this chosen ideal? This could be through brief moments of remembrance, looking at an inspiring

image, reading related texts, spending time in nature, or engaging in service aligned with that ideal. Journal your ideas.

(The path of Bhakti is a journey of the heart. By engaging in these practices with sincerity, you can deepen your loving connection with the Divine or your highest purpose, finding profound strength, joy, and guidance in your daily life.)

Part III: Living with Mastery – Your Path to Lasting Freedom (Adhyays 13-18)

Welcome to Part III, the culminating section of our journey through the Bhagavad Gita. In Part I, we laid the foundations, understanding our inner battlefield, the nature of the Self, and the initial paths of action, knowledge, and self-control. In Part II, we explored how to integrate this wisdom more deeply, understanding the Divine's pervasive presence and the power of devotion.

Now, in Part III, we delve into teachings that lead to true mastery – living with profound wisdom, unshakable equanimity, and lasting freedom. These final chapters offer a more analytical and comprehensive understanding of material nature, the forces that bind us (the Gunas), the nature of the Supreme Being, and the ultimate culmination of all spiritual paths in liberation (*Moksha*). This is where all the threads of knowledge, action, and devotion are woven together, guiding us towards becoming fully realized beings, living purposefully and freely in the world.

Adhyay 13: You Are the Watcher – Separating Self from Life's Drama

(Ksetra Ksetrajna Vibhaga Yoga – The Yoga of Differentiating the Field and its Knower)

Understanding the Arena of Life: Arjuna's Inquiry

Our journey through the Gita has revealed paths of action, knowledge, devotion, and meditation. We've glimpsed the awe-inspiring Universal Form of the Divine and the intimate path of the heart. Now, to deepen this understanding and pave the way for true mastery, Arjuna (in some recensions, or implicitly through the flow of Krishna's discourse) seeks knowledge about fundamental components of our existence. He inquires about *Prakriti* (material nature), *Purusha* (the spirit, the enjoyer), *Ksetra* (the field of activities, the body), and *Ksetrajna* (the knower of that field). He also asks about *Jnanam* (knowledge) and *Jneyam* (the object of knowledge).

Lord Krishna's response forms the essence of *Ksetra Ksetrajna Vibhaga Yoga*, the yoga of clearly distinguishing between the "field" of our material experience (our body-mind complex) and the "knower of the field" (our true Self, the soul or Atman). This chapter provides a profound analytical framework for understanding our reality, showing how mistaking one for the other is the root of our entanglement in life's drama, and how correctly differentiating them is the key to liberation. It's about understanding the stage, the actor & the observer.

Field vs. Knower: Differentiating Body & Experiences (Ksetra) from Your Eternal Self (Ksetrajna)

Krishna begins His explanation with clear definitions:

1. **The Ksetra (क्षेत्रम् – The Field):**

"This body, O son of Kuntī, is called the field." (BG 13.2). But the "field" is more than just the gross physical body:

- The five great elements (earth, water, fire, air, ether).
- The false ego (ahankara – the sense of "I-ness" associated with the body).
- The intellect (buddhi).
- The unmanifest (avyaktam – primordial material nature).
- The ten senses (five knowledge-acquiring senses: eyes, ears, nose, tongue, skin; and five working senses: voice, hands, legs, anus, genitals).
- The mind (manas).
- Five sense objects (sound, touch, form, taste, smell).
- It also includes desire, aversion, happiness, distress, the aggregate (the body as a whole), consciousness (as a symptom of life within the field, not the Ksetrajna itself), and fortitude.

In essence, the *Ksetra* encompasses our entire psycho-physical organism and the full spectrum of our material experiences, perceptions, thoughts, and emotions. It is the arena where our life's activities take place. It is temporary, constantly changing, and inert by itself (animated by the Ksetrajna).

2. **The Ksetrajna (क्षेत्रज्ञम् – The Knower of the Field):**

"And one who knows this body, O son of Kuntī, is called the knower of the field by those who know these things." (BG 13.2).

"You should understand that I (Krishna, as the Supersoul or Paramatma) am also the knower of the field in all bodies, O scion of Bharata." (BG 13.3). This implies that the individual soul (Atman) is also a knower of its own field, and Supreme (Paramatma) is the knower within all fields.

The *Ksetrajna* is the conscious principle, the pure awareness, the silent witness that observes and illuminates the field (the body and its experiences) but is inherently distinct from it. It is eternal, unchanging, and possesses consciousness as its very nature.

The Crucial Distinction: The fundamental teaching of this yoga is that true knowledge (*Jnanam*) lies in clearly understanding this distinction between the *Ksetra* and the *Ksetrajna*. Our suffering and bondage arise precisely because we mistakenly identify the Self (Ksetrajna) with the field (Ksetra). We think, "I *am* this body," "I *am* these thoughts," "I *am* these emotions," "I *am* these successes or failures." This misidentification leads to attachment, fear, and the endless drama of material existence. By realizing "I am the knower, the witness, separate from this ever-changing field," we begin to untangle ourselves.

Consciousness & Identity: Gaining Insights into the True Nature of Your Awareness

The *Ksetrajna*, the knower of the field, represents pure consciousness – the foundational awareness that makes all perception, thought, and experience possible. It is the light by which everything in the "field" is known. Yet, it remains untouched and unstained by the activities or qualities of the field, much like the sun illuminates the world but is not affected by the objects it shines upon.

Our everyday sense of identity is usually deeply invested in the *Ksetra*: "I am a manager in Mumbai," "I am a parent," "I am intelligent," "I am anxious," "I am healthy/sick." These are all descriptions of the field – roles, mental states, physical conditions. While these are part of our human experience, Jnana (true knowledge) involves recognizing that our ultimate identity, the "You" in the chapter title ("You Are the Watcher"), is the *Ksetrajna*, the silent, aware consciousness that witnesses all these passing shows.

This shift in identity from the temporary field to the eternal knower brings profound stability and peace because the knower is inherently:

Eternal and Unchanging: Unlike the body which ages or the mind which fluctuates.

Pure Awareness: Uncontaminated by the "dirt" of negative thoughts or emotions experienced within the field.

Inherently Peaceful: Its nature is peace, unlike the field which is often a place of turmoil.

To further illuminate this, Krishna also lists (BG 13.8-12) the qualities that constitute true knowledge (*Jnanam*). These include: humility, pridelessness, nonviolence, tolerance, simplicity, cleanliness, steadfastness, self-control, detachment from sense-objects, absence of false ego, clear perception of the evils of birth, death, old age, and disease, detachment to children, wife, home etc., and even-mindedness amid pleasant and unpleasant events. These virtues both arise from and support the understanding of the distinction between the Ksetra and Ksetrajna. They represent the mindset of one who is beginning to identify with the calm, observant Ksetrajna.

Transcending Limits: Practical Methods for Moving Beyond Perceived Physical or Mental Limitations

When our primary identification is with the *Ksetra* (the body-mind complex), we naturally feel constrained by its limitations. Physical illness, aging, mental distress, emotional turbulence, intellectual shortcomings – all these aspects of the field can seem to define and limit us, causing immense suffering.

However, when we begin to truly grasp and experientially realize, "I am the *Ksetrajna*, the knower, separate from this field," a profound shift occurs, empowering us to transcend these perceived limitations:

1. **Emotional Detachment & Resilience:** By cultivating the witness perspective, we can observe painful emotions (like anger, fear, sadness) arising within the "field" of our mind without being

completely overwhelmed or consumed by them. We can acknowledge, "There is anger arising in the mind-field," rather than "I *am* angry." This creates a space, reducing reactivity and fostering emotional resilience. Ksetrajna remains a calm observer.

2. **Reduced Fear of Physical Changes:** Understanding that the body is merely a temporary field, subject to birth, growth, decay, and death, helps to lessen the deep-seated fear associated with these natural processes. While we care for the body as a useful instrument, our core identity as the eternal Ksetrajna is not threatened by its changes.

3. **Mental Freedom and Cognitive Restructuring:** When we observe our thoughts as phenomena within the field, rather than as "who I am," we gain the freedom to question and change unhelpful or negative thought patterns. We are no longer slaves to every thought that arises; we can choose which thoughts to engage with.

4. **Increased Inner Stability & Peace:** By anchoring our identity in the unchanging Ksetrajna, we find a source of stability and peace that is independent of the ever-shifting circumstances of the field (external events, moods, physical states). We develop an inner sanctuary.

5. **Skillful Action (Karma Yoga Reinforcement):** This understanding allows us to act within the field (perform our duties) more effectively and with less

> stress, because we are not as desperately attached to the outcomes or as identified with the role of "doer."

The practical method for achieving this is the consistent practice of self-observation (*Sakshi Bhava*), consciously disidentifying from the contents of the field (body, thoughts, emotions) and reaffirming our identity as the silent, aware witness, the Ksetrajna.

Chapter 13 Takeaway: You Are the Silent Witness of Your Life's Play

The core teaching of Ksetra Ksetrajna Vibhaga Yoga is the liberating power of discrimination – clearly understanding the fundamental difference between the material body-mind complex (the Field, *Ksetra*) and the eternal, conscious Self (the Knower of the Field, *Ksetrajna*). This profound knowledge is the key to detaching from the ceaseless drama of material existence and recognizing our true identity as the silent, peaceful, and unchanging witness. By cultivating this "watcher" perspective, we begin to transcend perceived limitations, reduce suffering, and engage with life from a place of wisdom, freedom, and unshakable inner peace. This understanding is crucial as we move on to explore the forces (the Gunas) that animate the "field" itself.

इदं शरीरं कौन्तेय क्षेत्रमित्यभिधीयते । एतद्यो वेत्ति तं प्राहुः
क्षेत्रज्ञ इति तद्विदः ॥ १३.२ ॥ क्षेत्रज्ञं चापि मां विद्धि

सर्वक्षेत्रेषु भारत । क्षेत्रक्षेत्रज्ञयोर्ज्ञानं यत्तज्ज्ञानं मतं मम ॥ १३.३ ॥

Idaṁ śarīraṁ kaunteya kṣetram ity-abhidhīyate | Etad yo vetti taṁ prāhuḥ kṣetrajña iti tad-vidaḥ || 13.2 || Kṣetrajñaṁ cāpi māṁ viddhi sarva-kṣetreṣu bhārata | Kṣetra-kṣetrajñayor jñānaṁ yat taj-jñānaṁ mataṁ mama || 13.3 ||

Hindi (13.2-3): "हे कौन्तेय! यह शरीर 'क्षेत्र' इस नाम से कहा जाता है और इसको जो जानता है, उसको 'क्षेत्रज्ञ' ऐसा उन दोनों के तत्त्व को जानने वाले ज्ञानीजन कहते हैं। हे भारत! सब क्षेत्रों में क्षेत्रज्ञ मुझे ही जान और क्षेत्र-क्षेत्रज्ञ का जो ज्ञान है, वही ज्ञान है – ऐसा मेरा मत है।"

English (13.2-3): "This body, O son of Kuntī, is called the field, and one who knows this body is called the knower of the field by those who know of these things. O scion of Bharata, you should understand that I am also the knower of the field in all bodies, and to understand this field and its knower is called knowledge. That is my opinion." ***(These verses establish the fundamental definitions of the Field (Ksetra) and the Knower of the Field (Ksetrajna), and declare that understanding them constitutes true knowledge.)***

Exercise: Self-Observation – Cultivating the 'Watcher' Perspective

These practices are designed to help you experientially differentiate between the "field" (your body, thoughts, emotions) and the "knower of the field" (your true Self as the observer), fostering healthy detachment.

1. **Practice: Observing the 'Field' Within (10-15 minutes):**

Settle and Scan: Sit quietly and comfortably. Take a few gentle breaths.

Body as Field: Bring your awareness to your physical body. Notice any sensations – areas of comfort, discomfort, tension, warmth, coolness, the feeling of your breath. Silently acknowledge: "This body and its sensations are the field; I am the awareness observing this field."

Thoughts as Field: Shift your attention to your thoughts. Watch them as they arise and pass, like clouds in the sky or images on a screen. Don't engage with them, judge them, or try to stop them. Silently acknowledge: "These thoughts are arising and passing within the field of my mind; I am the awareness observing these thoughts."

Emotions as Field: Become aware of any emotions present – perhaps calmness, restlessness, subtle joy, or a hint of worry. Notice the feeling tone and any associated physical sensations. Silently acknowledge: "These emotions are experiences within the field; I am the awareness observing these emotions."

Rest as the Knower: For the last few minutes, simply rest in the identity of the silent, peaceful observer – the Ksetrajna – that is aware of all these changing phenomena within the field of your experience.

2. **Practice: Disidentifying from a Dominant Role or Identity (10 minutes reflection/journaling):**

Choose a Role: Select one significant role you play in your life (e.g., "employee," "parent," "student," "friend," "artist") or a strong aspect of your current identity (e.g., "achiever," "helper," "anxious person").

Analyze as 'Field': Reflect on or journal about how this role/identity is part of your 'Ksetra' (field).

- What specific thoughts, emotions, behaviors, and expectations are associated with this role/identity?
- How does this role/identity change over time or in different situations?
- In what ways do you sometimes over-identify with this role, leading to stress or limitations?

Adopt the 'Knower' Perspective: Now, try to view this role/identity from the detached perspective of the Ksetrajna (the calm, aware, unchanging Self). How would the Ksetrajna perceive this role and its associated experiences?

Would it be less burdened by the pressures or outcomes associated with that role? What wisdom or peace might arise from this observer perspective?

3. **Reflection Practice: Identifying a 'Field-Knower' Distinction Moment:**

Recall: Think about your day so far or yesterday. Identify one specific moment where you felt particularly caught up in or reactive to your thoughts, emotions, or a physical sensation (the 'field'). Perhaps you felt stressed by a thought, upset by an emotion, or overly concerned about a physical discomfort.

Apply the Distinction: Now, reflect on that same moment. How could you have, even briefly, remembered yourself as the 'Knower' (Ksetrajna), the silent witness to that experience within the field? What might have changed in your inner state or your response if you had been able to create that small space of awareness between the 'Knower' and the 'Field'? Journal your insights.

(Cultivating the 'Watcher' perspective is a powerful practice for inner freedom. With consistency, you'll find it easier to navigate life's dramas with greater peace and wisdom, knowing your true Self remains untouched.)

Adhyay 14: Master Your Inner Energy – Navigate Life's Underlying Forces

(Gunatraya Vibhaga Yoga – The Yoga of the Division of the Three Modes)

The Invisible Threads: How Nature Conditions Us

In Adhyay 13, Lord Krishna provided a deep analytical understanding of the "field" (*Ksetra* – our body-mind complex) and the "knower of the field" (*Ksetrajna* – our true Self, the Atman). We learned that true wisdom lies in differentiating the conscious Self from the material field it inhabits. A natural question then arises: If the Self is eternal and distinct, how does it become entangled and conditioned within this material field, experiencing joy, sorrow, and the drama of life?

Krishna now reveals the answer by explaining the workings of the three *Gunas* – the fundamental modes or qualities of material nature (*Prakriti*). These Gunas – Sattva (goodness/clarity), Rajas (passion/activity), and Tamas (ignorance/inertia) – are like invisible energetic threads that emanate from Prakriti and bind the immortal soul, the Ksetrajna, to the Ksetra. Understanding these underlying forces is crucial for navigating life with awareness, cultivating inner balance, and ultimately transcending their powerful influence to achieve true freedom. This chapter, *Gunatraya Vibhaga Yoga*, is our guide to mastering these inner energies.

Decoding the Three Gunas: Understanding Sattva (Clarity), Rajas (Passion), Tamas (Inertia)

The three Gunas are subtle, pervasive qualities that constitute the fabric of material nature and influence every aspect of our existence – our physical state, mental disposition, emotional responses, actions, and even our understanding of the world. They are constantly interacting and competing for dominance within us and in the environment around us.

1. Sattva Guna (Mode of Goodness/Clarity/Harmony):

- **Characteristics:** Sattva is characterized by purity, illumination, knowledge, wisdom, harmony, peace, happiness, contentment, virtue, and a sense of well-being. It promotes clarity of thought, calmness of mind, and a natural inclination towards goodness and spiritual understanding. When Sattva is dominant, one feels light, joyful, and connected.
- **How it Binds:** While Sattva is the purest of the three and highly conducive to spiritual progress, it can still bind the soul through a subtle attachment to the happiness and knowledge it brings. One might develop a refined ego based on being "good," "knowledgeable," or "happy," creating a subtle form of bondage if not transcended.

2. Rajas Guna (Mode of Passion/Activity/Attachment):

- **Characteristics:** Rajas is born of intense longing, craving, and attachment. It manifests as dynamic activity, ambition, restlessness, greed, passion, competition, and a strong desire for the fruits of one's actions. When Rajas is dominant, one feels driven, energetic, and often agitated, constantly striving for more – more possessions, more recognition, more sensory pleasure.

- **How it Binds:** Rajas binds the soul through its insatiable desires and attachment to action and its results. This leads to a cycle of intense effort, temporary gratification, inevitable frustration when desires are unfulfilled, and a perpetual state of unrest and discontent.

3. Tamas Guna (Mode of Ignorance/Inertia/Darkness):

- **Characteristics:** Tamas is born of ignorance and delusion. It manifests as darkness, inertia, laziness, lethargy, procrastination, confusion, carelessness, excessive sleep, apathy, and a lack of discrimination. When Tamas is dominant, one feels heavy, dull, unmotivated, and disconnected from reality, often leading to negligence and harmful behavior.
- **How it Binds:** Tamas binds the soul by obscuring knowledge, fostering illusion, and leading to inaction or inappropriate action. It veils the true nature of the Self and the world, keeping one trapped in a cycle of confusion and despair.

It's crucial to understand that these three Gunas are always present in varying proportions in every individual and every aspect of material existence. They are in a constant state of flux, one Guna temporarily overpowering the others, leading to shifts in our moods, thoughts, and behaviors.

How Gunas Shape You: Recognizing Their Influence on Your Thoughts, Emotions, Actions

The interplay of these three Gunas profoundly shapes our entire experience of life. Recognizing their influence is the first step toward gaining some mastery over them:

Influence on Thoughts:

- **Sattvic Thoughts:** Clear, positive, insightful, focused on truth and wisdom, leading to understanding and peace.
- **Rajasic Thoughts:** Agitated, filled with desires and plans, critical, judgmental, restless, jumping from one idea to another.
- **Tamasic Thoughts:** Dull, confused, negative, fearful, based on illusion or misinformation, leading to misunderstanding and inaction.

Influence on Emotions:

- **Sattvic Emotions:** Peacefulness, joy, contentment, compassion, love, empathy, fearlessness.
- **Rajasic Emotions:** Anger, anxiety, greed, frustration, envy, impatience, intense craving, excitement.
- **Tamasic Emotions:** Depression, apathy, hopelessness, overwhelming fear, grief, laziness, shame.

Influence on Actions & Behavior:

- **Sattvic Actions:** Purposeful, ethical, performed with care and attention, balanced, for the welfare of others, leading to positive outcomes.
- **Rajasic Actions:** Frenzied, competitive, driven by ambition or passion, often for selfish gain, leading to stress and agitation.
- **Tamasic Actions:** Characterized by lethargy, procrastination, negligence, destructive tendencies, or actions performed without considering consequences.

Influence on Lifestyle Choices: Even our preferences are shaped by the Gunas:

- **Food:** Sattvic foods are fresh, juicy, nourishing, and promote health and clarity (e.g., fruits, vegetables, grains, dairy). Rajasic foods are overly spicy, salty, or stimulating, leading to agitation (e.g., chilies, coffee, heavily processed foods). Tamasic foods are stale, impure, or intoxicating, leading to dullness (e.g., overcooked/leftover food, meat, alcohol).
- **Work, Sleep, Entertainment:** The type of work we are drawn to, our sleep patterns, and our choices of entertainment also reflect our dominant Gunas.

By observing our own thoughts, emotions, actions, and preferences through the lens of the Gunas, we can gain invaluable self-awareness. This is not about labeling ourselves as "good" or "bad," but about understanding the underlying energies at play so we can make more conscious choices.

Cultivating Inner Balance: Strategies to Enhance Sattva & Reduce Rajas/Tamas

While the ultimate spiritual goal is to transcend all three Gunas and become a *Gunatita* (one beyond the modes), Krishna explains that for most seekers, the practical first step is to consciously **increase Sattva Guna** in their lives. Sattva provides the clarity, peace, and stability necessary for deeper spiritual understanding and practice. It acts like a clear window, allowing the light of the Self to shine through.

Strategies to Increase Sattva:

- **Sattvic Diet:** Prioritize fresh, wholesome, plant-based foods that are pure, light, and nourishing. Eat mindfully and in moderation.
- **Sattvic Environment:** Create a clean, orderly, peaceful, and harmonious living and working space. Spend time in nature, which is inherently Sattvic.
- **Sattvic Activities & Company (Satsanga):** Engage in activities that promote knowledge, peace, and well-being – such as studying wisdom texts (like this one!), meditation, yoga, selfless service (Seva), spending time with spiritually uplifting people, and engaging in work that feels meaningful and ethical.
- **Sattvic Thoughts & Speech:** Consciously cultivate positive thinking, truthfulness, kindness in speech, and avoid gossip or harsh words.

- **Regulated Lifestyle:** Maintain regular and moderate habits in sleep, work, and recreation.

Strategies to Reduce Rajas:

- **Practice Moderation:** Be mindful of excessive ambition, activity, and sensory stimulation. Cultivate contentment.

- **Mindfulness & Calm:** Use mindfulness practices to observe and calm restless thoughts and impulses.

- **Detachment (Karma Yoga):** Focus on performing your duty well, without excessive attachment to specific outcomes or rewards.

- **Avoid Overstimulation:** Limit exposure to agitating environments, aggressive entertainment, or excessive caffeine/stimulants.

Strategies to Reduce Tamas:

- **Embrace Activity:** Engage in regular physical exercise and purposeful activity, even when you don't feel like it initially.

- **Seek Knowledge & Clarity:** Actively challenge ignorance and delusion by seeking out inspiring and illuminating knowledge.

- **Mindful Consumption:** Avoid excessive sleep, intoxicating substances, dulling entertainment, and impure or stale food.

- **Maintain Routine:** Establishing a regular daily routine can help counteract lethargy and procrastination.
- **Positive Association:** Seek the company of energetic, positive, and motivated individuals.

By consciously making choices that favor Sattva, we create an inner environment more conducive to peace, clarity, and spiritual growth, making it easier to then rise above the influence of Rajas and Tamas.

Transcending the Gunas – The Path to True Freedom

While increasing Sattva is beneficial, Krishna makes it clear that even Sattva binds the soul through attachment to happiness and knowledge. True liberation (*Moksha*) means becoming a *Gunatita* – one who has completely transcended the influence of all three Gunas.

Krishna describes the characteristics of such a liberated soul (BG 14.22-25):

- **Equanimity:** They are not disturbed when illumination (Sattva), activity (Rajas), or delusion (Tamas) are present, nor do they long for them when they are absent.
- **Neutrality (The Witness):** They remain like a neutral observer, understanding that it is only the Gunas (the modes of nature) that are interacting with their objects, and the Self is distinct. They are not swayed.

- **Established in the Self:** They are firmly situated in their true spiritual nature, undisturbed by the play of the Gunas.
- **Equal Vision:** They regard pleasure and pain, a clod of earth, a stone, and gold with an equal eye. They are the same towards the agreeable and the disagreeable, praise and blame, honor and dishonor, friends and enemies.
- **Renunciation of Selfish Undertakings:** They have renounced all undertakings driven by selfish desire or ego.

How does one achieve this state of transcendence? Krishna gives a clear and direct answer: *"One who engages in full devotional service (Bhakti Yoga), unfailing in all circumstances, at once transcends the modes of material nature and thus comes to the level of Brahman."* (BG 14.26). Unwavering, loving devotion to the Supreme Lord is presented as the most effective means to rise above the influence of the Gunas and realize one's eternal, spiritual nature.

Chapter 14 Takeaway: Navigating Life's Energies with Wisdom

Understanding the three Gunas – Sattva, Rajas, and Tamas – provides an incredibly insightful and practical framework for navigating the complexities of our inner and outer worlds. By recognizing how these fundamental energies shape our thoughts, emotions, actions, and choices, we gain the power of self-awareness. The path involves consciously cultivating

Sattva to create clarity and peace, mindfully reducing the grip of Rajas and Tamas, and ultimately, aiming to transcend all three modes, primarily through unwavering devotional service. This mastery over our inner energies is not about suppression, but about aligning ourselves with our true spiritual nature, leading to a life of balance, purpose, and lasting freedom from the conditioning of material nature.

मां च योऽव्यभिचारेण भक्तियोगेन सेवते । स गुणान्समतीत्यैतान्ब्रह्मभूयाय कल्पते ॥ १४.२६ ॥

Māṁ ca yo 'vyabhicāreṇa bhakti-yogena sevate | Sa guṇān samatītyaitān brahma-bhūyāya kalpate || 14.26 ||

Hindi: "और जो कोई अव्यभिचारी भक्तियोग के द्वारा मेरी सेवा करता है, वह इन गुणों को लाँघकर ब्रह्मपद को प्राप्त होने योग्य हो जाता है।"

English: "One who engages in full devotional service, unfailing in all circumstances, at once transcends the modes of material nature and thus comes to the level of Brahman." ***(This verse clearly states that unswerving devotional service is the means to transcend the three Gunas.)***

Exercise: Identifying & Balancing the Gunas Within You

These practices will help you become more aware of the play of the Gunas in your life and take conscious steps towards cultivating greater Sattva and balance.

1. Practice: Guna Self-Assessment – A Weekly Review:

At the end of each day for a week, or once at the end of the week, take 15-20 minutes to reflect. Consider the following areas of your life for that period:

- **Diet:** What kinds of food did you predominantly eat? (Fresh/Wholesome vs. Spicy/Stimulating vs. Stale/Heavy)
- **Work/Study Style:** How did you approach your tasks? (Calm/Focused vs. Frenzied/Stressed vs. Procrastinating/Dull)
- **Leisure/Entertainment:** What activities did you engage in for relaxation? (Peaceful/Uplifting vs. Agitating/Overstimulating vs. Mind-Numbing/Lethargic)
- **Dominant Moods/Emotions:** What feelings were most prevalent? (Peace/Joy vs. Anxiety/Anger vs. Sadness/Apathy)
- **Reactions to Stress/Challenges:** How did you typically respond to difficulties? (With equanimity vs. with agitation/aggression vs. with withdrawal/despair)
- **Sleep Quality:** Was your sleep restful and refreshing, disturbed and restless, or excessive and leading to dullness?

Journal: For each area, try to identify which Guna (Sattva, Rajas, or Tamas) seemed most influential. Note any patterns you observe. There's no judgment here, only awareness.

2. Practice: Crafting a Sattva-Boosting Action Plan:

Based on your Guna Self-Assessment, identify one or two specific areas where you'd like to consciously increase Sattva (or reduce Rajas/Tamas).

Create a Small, Actionable Plan: For each area, define 1-2 concrete, achievable steps you can take in the coming week.

- *Example for Diet:* "I will include at least two servings of fresh fruit in my daily meals." or "I will reduce my coffee intake by one cup."
- *Example for Leisure:* "I will dedicate 15 minutes to quiet reading or meditation before bed instead of scrolling on social media."
- *Example for Reactions:* "When I feel stressed, I will take three deep breaths before responding."

Track & Review: At the end of the week, review how you did with your plan. What worked? What was challenging? Adjust your plan for the following week if needed.

3. Reflection Practice: Observing Gunas in Specific Situations:

Recall: Think of a specific recent situation where you felt particularly agitated and driven (likely Rajasic dominance)

OR a situation where you felt notably dull, unmotivated, or confused (likely Tamasic dominance).

Analyze:

- What were the internal or external triggers?
- How did this dominant Guna affect your thoughts, words, and actions in that moment?
- What were the consequences, for yourself & others?
- If you could replay that situation with a more Sattvic mindset, what might you have thought, said, or done differently? How might that have changed the outcome or your inner experience? Journal

4. Reflection Practice: The Path to Transcendence Through Devotion:

Lord Krishna states (BG 14.26) that unwavering devotional service (Bhakti Yoga) helps one transcend the three Gunas.

Contemplate: How do you personally understand this connection? In what ways could cultivating a deeper, loving relationship with the Divine (or your highest spiritual ideal/purpose) help you to:

- Rise above the subtle attachment to Sattvic happiness and knowledge?
- Reduce the pull of Rajasic desires and restless activity?
- Dispel the darkness and inertia of Tamas?

Journal any thoughts or feelings that arise about how devotion might be a practical path for you to move beyond the influence of the Gunas.

(Understanding & working with the Gunas is a lifelong journey of self-discovery. Be patient and compassionate with yourself as you practice these awareness techniques.)

Adhyay 15: Connect to the Source – Realizing Your Link to the Highest

(Purushottama Yoga – The Yoga of the Supreme Person)

Beyond the Illusions: Seeking the Ultimate Reality

In Adhyay 14, Lord Krishna provided a crucial understanding of the three Gunas – Sattva, Rajas, and Tamas – the subtle forces of material nature that bind us to the cycle of existence. We learned how these modes influence our thoughts, actions, and experiences, and how, through conscious effort and devotion, we can begin to transcend their sway. Now, to further illuminate the path to ultimate freedom, Krishna introduces *Purushottama Yoga*, the yoga of understanding the Supreme Person, who is the ultimate source, sustainer, and controller of both the material and spiritual worlds. He uses the powerful metaphor of an imperishable, yet entangling, banyan tree to describe the nature of this material world and reveals how, by understanding its true root and cultivating detachment, we can connect with Him, the Supreme Purushottama.

The Entangling Tree of Material Existence (The Ashvattha Tree Analogy)

Krishna begins with a striking allegory to illustrate the nature of our entanglement in the material world:

"They speak of an imperishable banyan tree (Ashvattha) having its roots upward and its branches down; its leaves are the Vedic hymns. One who knows this tree is the knower of the Vedas." (BG 15.1, paraphrased)

This metaphorical tree represents the entirety of material existence (*samsara*):

- **Roots Upward:** Its roots extend upwards because its ultimate origin and source is the Supreme Being, in the spiritual realm. This material world is a reflection, albeit a temporary and often distorted one, of that higher reality.

- **Branches Downward:** Its branches spread downwards and outwards, representing the expansion of the cosmos and the myriad forms of life and experiences within it, across different planetary systems and species.

- **Leaves as Vedic Hymns:** The leaves are compared to the ritualistic sections of the Vedas, which prescribe activities for material gain, thereby nourishing the tree's growth and keeping beings entangled in worldly pursuits if performed with attachment.

- **Nourished by the Gunas:** The twigs of this tree are the sense objects, and its growth is nourished by the three Gunas (Sattva, Rajas, Tamas), which fuel our desires and actions within this world.

- **Perpetuating Entanglement:** The branches lead to further entanglement as beings engage in sense gratification, leading to repeated birth and death. The true form of this tree – its beginning, its end, and its real foundation – is not easily perceived by those caught within its intricate web.

This Ashvattha tree symbolizes the alluring yet ultimately temporary and binding nature of material existence. We are like birds flitting from branch to branch, seeking fleeting pleasures, often unaware of the tree's true source or the way out of its entanglement.

Seeking the Primal Source – Beyond the Entanglement: The Axe of Detachment

How does one escape this vast, entangling tree of material life? Krishna provides a clear directive:

"This deeply rooted Ashvattha tree should be cut down with the strong weapon of detachment (asanga-shastrena)." (BG 15.3, paraphrased)

Detachment (*asanga* or *vairagya*), cultivated through the practices described in earlier chapters (Karma Yoga, Jnana Yoga, Dhyana Yoga), is the axe that severs our binding attachments to the sense objects and temporary pleasures offered by this material world.

Once these roots of attachment are cut, Krishna advises that one must then seek out that primeval source, that ultimate abode, "from which, having gone, they never return." This is the spiritual realm, the eternal abode of the Supreme Person. To reach this state, one needs specific qualifications:

- **Freedom from Illusion and False Prestige:** Overcoming the ego's delusions and the pride associated with temporary material achievements.

- **Conquering False Association:** Understanding that our true association is with the eternal Self and the Supreme, not just with temporary material relationships or identities.
- **Understanding the Eternal:** Dwelling on the nature of the eternal Self and the Supreme.
- **Cessation of Material Lust:** Overcoming the powerful drive for selfish sensory gratification.
- **Freedom from Dualities:** Becoming free from the influence of worldly dualities like happiness and distress, pleasure and pain.
- **Knowing How to Surrender:** Unbewildered, knowing how to surrender unto that Supreme Person.

Krishna describes His supreme abode as a self-luminous realm, not illuminated by the sun, moon, or fire. Once an individual soul reaches that abode, they do not return to this cycle of material existence.

Understanding the Supreme: Connecting with the Highest Aspect of Consciousness or the Divine (Purushottama Defined)

To clarify the nature of this ultimate goal and the Supreme Person who presides over it, Krishna explains the concept of *Purushottama*:

1. **Kshara Purusha (The Fallible/Perishable):** These are all living beings within the material world, bound

by the Gunas and subject to change and the cycle of birth and death. Their bodies are perishable.

2. **Akshara Purusha (The Infallible/Imperishable):** This refers to the collective of liberated souls who reside in the spiritual realm, or sometimes to the unmanifest, undifferentiated spiritual energy (Brahman). These are unchanging and eternal.

3. **Purushottama (The Supreme Person):** Beyond both the fallible (kshara) and the infallible (akshara) is the highest person, the Supreme Self, known as Purushottama. He is the transcendental Lord (Ishvara) who enters the three worlds and maintains them all. He is superior to both the conditioned souls and the liberated souls, being the ultimate source and controller of everything.

Krishna emphatically declares: *"Because I am transcendental, beyond both the fallible and the infallible, and because I am the greatest, I am celebrated both in the world and in the Vedas as that Supreme Person (Purushottama)."* (BG 15.18).

One who, without delusion, knows Him as this Supreme Person, knows everything. Such a person, Krishna says, engages in His loving devotional service (Bhakti Yoga) with their whole being. This understanding of the Purushottama is the most confidential part of the Vedic scriptures, and understanding it makes one wise and their endeavors perfect.

Your Place in the Cosmos: The Relationship Between Your Individual Soul & the Supreme

Krishna further clarifies the intimate and eternal relationship between the individual soul (*jiva-atma*) and Himself, the Supreme Soul (Paramatma or Purushottama):

"The living entities in this conditioned world are My eternal, fragmental parts (mamaivamsho jiva-loke jiva-bhutah sanatanah)." (BG 15.7).

This profound statement reveals:

- **Eternal Connection:** We, as individual souls, are not accidentally created or temporarily existent; we are eternally connected to the Supreme.

- **Qualitative Oneness, Quantitative Difference:** As fragmental parts, we share the spiritual quality of the Supreme (consciousness, eternality, bliss) but are quantitatively minute. We are like sparks of fire – possessing the quality of fire, but not the fire itself.

- **The Struggle in Material Nature:** Though eternally spiritual, the soul, when in material world, becomes covered by material nature and struggles with six senses, which include the mind. It is these senses that pull the soul towards temporary material experiences.

- **Transmigration:** The soul carries its subtle body (mind, intelligence, ego) and its acquired conceptions of life from one physical body to another, just as the air carries aromas.

- **The Lord as the Inner Sustainer:** Krishna also explains His role as the indwelling Paramatma, the

> Supersoul, who sustains all life. He states: "I enter into each planet, and by My energy they stay in orbit. I become the moon and thereby supply the juice of life to all vegetables." (BG 15.13). Furthermore, "I am the fire of digestion in the bodies of all living entities, and I join with the air of life, outgoing and incoming, to digest the four kinds of foodstuff." (BG 15.14). And most importantly, *"I am seated in everyone's heart, and from Me come remembrance, knowledge, and forgetfulness."* (BG 15.15).

This understanding establishes our inherent, unbreakable link with the Supreme Person. We are never truly alone or disconnected; the Supreme Source is always within us and all around us, sustaining our very existence. Recognizing this connection is key to realizing our spiritual potential.

Inspired Connection: Learning from Stories of Spiritual Leaders Who Embodied This Link

Many spiritual luminaries throughout history have lived lives that powerfully demonstrated this profound personal connection with the Purushottama, the Supreme Person. Their experiences often highlight an unwavering faith in, and loving dedication to, this ultimate source.

Sant Jnaneshwar (India, 13th Century): A revered poet-saint from Maharashtra, Jnaneshwar, in his commentary on the Gita (Jnaneshwari), beautifully expounded on the personal and all-pervading nature of the Supreme. His life, though short, was filled with a deep mystical connection and a mission to make profound spiritual truths accessible through the common language, embodying a life lived in constant awareness of this divine link.

Sri Ramanujacharya (India, 11th-12th Century): A prominent philosopher-saint, Ramanujacharya championed the philosophy of Vishishtadvaita (qualified non-dualism), which emphasizes the reality of the Supreme Person (Narayana/Vishnu) as the ultimate reality, with individual souls being His eternal parts, distinct yet inseparable. His life was dedicated to establishing temples, standardizing worship, and propagating the path of loving devotion (Bhakti) as the means to connect with the Purushottama.

Countless Devotees: Beyond famous names, countless individuals from various traditions have experienced and expressed this personal link through their simple faith, heartfelt prayers, and lives of service and devotion, showing that this connection is not limited to great scholars or ascetics but is available to any sincere heart.

These examples show that the concept of Purushottama is not just a philosophical abstraction but can be a living, breathing reality, guiding and inspiring a life of profound connection and purpose.

Chapter 15 Takeaway: You Are Eternally Connected to the Supreme Source

Purushottama Yoga offers one of the most profound and complete understandings of reality presented in the Bhagavad Gita. It reveals the Supreme Person, Lord Krishna, as the ultimate source, sustainer, and goal of all existence, transcendental to both the perishable material world and the imperishable individual souls. By understanding the metaphorical tree of material existence and the means to detach from it – through knowledge and unwavering devotion – we can realize our true nature as eternal fragmental parts of this Supreme Person. This realization frees us from illusion, empowers us to live with wisdom and purpose, and ultimately leads us back to our eternal home in the spiritual realm, a state of everlasting bliss and connection.

यस्मात्क्षरमतीतोऽहमक्षरादपि चोत्तमः । अतोऽस्मि लोके वेदे च प्रथितः पुरुषोत्तमः ॥ १५.१८ ॥

Yasmāt kṣaram-atīto 'ham-akṣarād-api cottamaḥ | Ato 'smi loke vede ca prathitaḥ puruṣottamaḥ || 15.18 ||

Hindi: "क्योंकि मैं क्षर (नाशवान् जड़वर्ग) से अतीत हूँ और अक्षर (अविनाशी जीवात्मा) से भी उत्तम हूँ, इसलिये लोक में और वेद में पुरुषोत्तम नाम से प्रसिद्ध हूँ।"

English: "Because I am transcendental, beyond both the fallible (kshara) and the infallible (akshara), and because I am the greatest, I am celebrated both in the world and in the Vedas as that Supreme Person (Purushottama)." ***(This verse directly declares Krishna's identity as the Purushottama, the Supreme Person.)***

Exercise: Techniques for Developing a Personal Relationship and Connection with the Divine/Source

These exercises are designed to help you reflect on your connection with the Supreme Source and cultivate a more personal relationship.

1. **Practice: Seeing the Divine Sustenance (5-10 minutes reflection):**

Choose an Element: Select one essential aspect of life that sustains you – it could be the sunlight that warms the earth, the air you breathe, the water you drink, the food you eat, or even the faculty of digestion within your body.

Contemplate the Source: Reflect on Krishna's teachings in this chapter (e.g., BG 15.12-14) where He states He is the energy behind these phenomena (the light of the sun, the fire of digestion, the sustainer of planets).

Cultivate Gratitude & Connection: As you contemplate, try to feel a sense of gratitude not just for the element itself, but for the Supreme Source that provides and sustains it. Acknowledge this divine support in your life.

2. **Practice: Affirming Your Eternal Connection (5 minutes daily):**

Affirmation: Spend a few minutes each day, perhaps upon waking or before sleeping, silently or softly repeating an affirmation based on BG 15.7: "I am an eternal spiritual being, a part of the Supreme Source. My true nature is consciousness and joy."

Feel Into It: Don't just repeat the words mechanically. Try to feel the meaning and implications of this statement. Let it sink into your awareness.

3. **Reflection Practice: Identifying and 'Cutting' an Attachment Root:**

The Gita (BG 15.3) advises cutting the deeply rooted "Ashvattha tree" of material existence with the "strong weapon of detachment."

Identify a 'Root': Reflect on one specific attachment in your life that you feel strongly binds you or causes you distress when threatened (e.g., attachment to a particular outcome at work, to a specific person's approval, to a material possession, to your physical appearance, or to a specific comfort).

Consider 'Detachment': What would it *practically mean* to apply the "axe of detachment" to this specific root? It doesn't necessarily mean abandoning the thing/person, but rather changing your inner relationship to it – reducing dependency, letting go of obsessive craving, accepting impermanence.

Small Step: What is one small, conscious step you could take this week to practice this detachment in relation to that specific root? Journal your thoughts.

4. **Reflection Practice: Personalizing Your Connection with the 'Purushottama':**

Lord Krishna reveals Himself as the Purushottama, the Supreme Person, who is the source of remembrance, knowledge, and forgetfulness, and is seated in everyone's heart (BG 15.15).

Qualities that Resonate: Which qualities of the Supreme Person (e.g., as loving sustainer, ultimate controller, source of all wisdom, compassionate guide, inner friend) resonate most deeply with you personally?

Cultivating Relationship: How can you begin to cultivate a more personal sense of relationship or connection with this Supreme Person, focusing on the qualities that inspire you? This might involve prayer, talking to Him in your heart, offering your actions, or simply remembering His presence. Journal your ideas on making this connection more real and personal for you.

(By contemplating these truths and engaging in these practices, you begin to shift your identity from the temporary entanglements of the material world to your eternal, loving relationship with the Supreme Person, the ultimate source of all existence and lasting fulfillment.)

Adhyay 16: Choose Your Higher Path – Transforming Habits, Cultivating Virtues

(Daivasura Sampad Vibhaga Yoga – The Yoga of the Division between Divine and Demoniac Natures)

The Inner Compass: Aligning with Our Divine Potential

Having understood the Supreme Person (Purushottama) as the ultimate reality in Adhyay 15, a practical question arises: What kind of inner disposition and conduct aligns us with this Supreme Truth, and what kind leads us away from it? Lord Krishna now addresses this by meticulously detailing two fundamental human natures or temperaments: the divine (*Daivi Sampad*) and the demoniac (*Asuri Sampad*). These are not merely labels for different types of people, but represent sets of qualities and worldviews that exist, to varying degrees, within all of us.

This chapter, *Daivasura Sampad Vibhaga Yoga*, serves as a clear mirror, helping us identify these contrasting tendencies within ourselves. It illuminates how divine qualities pave the path to liberation, peace, and our true spiritual nature, while demoniac traits lead to bondage, suffering, and repeated entanglement in the material world. Understanding this division empowers us to consciously choose our higher path, transforming detrimental habits and actively cultivating the virtues that reflect our inherent divinity.

Divine vs. Demoniac: Understanding the Contrasting Qualities (Virtues vs. Hindrances) Within Us

Lord Krishna begins by enumerating the qualities characteristic of those endowed with a **Divine Nature**

(Daivi Sampad), qualities that are conducive to spiritual progress and ultimate liberation (BG 16.1-3):

- **Fearlessness (Abhayam):** True courage born from understanding one's eternal nature and trusting in the Divine.
- **Purification of One's Existence (Sattva-samshuddhi):** Purity of heart, mind, and actions.
- **Cultivation of Spiritual Knowledge (Jnana-yoga-vyavasthiti):** Steadfastness in the pursuit and application of spiritual wisdom.
- **Charity (Danam):** Generosity, giving freely without expecting return.
- **Self-Control (Dama):** Control over the external senses.
- **Performance of Sacrifice (Yajna):** Performing actions for a higher purpose, as an offering.
- **Study of Sacred Scriptures (Svadhyaya):** Engaging with wisdom texts.
- **Austerity (Tapa):** Voluntary self-discipline for purification and spiritual growth.
- **Simplicity/Straightforwardness (Arjavam):** Honesty and directness in thought, word, and deed.
- **Nonviolence (Ahimsa):** Not causing harm to any living being in thought, word, or deed.

- **Truthfulness (Satyam):** Adherence to truth, speaking truthfully and kindly.
- **Freedom from Anger (Akrodha):** Maintaining calmness even when provoked.
- **Renunciation (Tyaga):** Detachment from selfish desires and the fruits of action.
- **Tranquility (Shanti):** Inner peace and serenity.
- **Aversion to Fault-Finding (Apaishunam):** Refraining from speaking ill of others.
- **Compassion for All Living Entities (Daya Bhuteshu):** Kindness and empathy towards all beings.
- **Freedom from Covetousness (Aloluptvam):** Not being greedy or possessive; contentment with what one has.
- **Gentleness (Mardavam):** Softness of heart, kindness in demeanor.
- **Modesty (Hri):** Humility, a sense of shame in performing improper actions.
- **Steady Determination (Achapalam):** Freedom from fickleness, steadfastness in purpose.
- **Vigor/Radiance (Tejah):** Spiritual strength and inner luminosity.

- **Forgiveness (Kshama):** The ability to pardon offenses.
- **Fortitude (Dhriti):** Patience and perseverance, especially in adversity.
- **Cleanliness (Shaucham):** External and internal purity.
- **Freedom from Envy (Adroha):** Not feeling malice or ill-will towards others.
- **Freedom from the Passion for Honor (Na-atimanita):** Not craving respect or adulation from others.

These twenty-six qualities, Krishna states, belong to pious souls endowed with a divine nature and are conducive to liberation.

In stark contrast, He then describes the qualities marking the **Demoniac Nature (Asuri Sampad)** (BG 16.4):

- **Ostentation/Pretense (Dambha):** Hypocrisy, making a show of virtue or piety one doesn't possess.
- **Arrogance/Pride (Darpa):** Haughtiness stemming from wealth, education, lineage, etc.
- **Self-Conceit/Excessive Pride (Abhimana):** An inflated sense of one's own importance, vanity.
- **Anger (Krodha):** Wrathfulness, irritability, and a tendency towards rage.

- **Harshness (Parushyam):** Cruelty in speech and action.
- **Ignorance (Ajnanam):** Lack of discrimination between right and wrong, spiritual blindness.

These demoniac qualities, Krishna explains, inevitably lead to entanglement and bondage in the material world.

Recognizing Growth Paths: Consequences, Worldviews, and the Importance of Guidance

Lord Krishna leaves no doubt about the outcomes of these two natures: *"The divine qualities lead to liberation, O son of Pandu, whereas the demoniac qualities lead to bondage."* (BG 16.5). He then provides a detailed and sobering analysis of the worldview and behavior of those dominated by demoniac tendencies (BG 16.7-20):

- **Lack of Moral Compass:** They do not understand what action should be performed and what should be avoided. Cleanliness, proper conduct, and truthfulness are absent in them.
- **Materialistic Worldview:** They assert that the world is unreal, without any foundation or divine controller, born merely of sexual desire, with no cause other than lust.
- **Destructive Actions:** Holding such nihilistic views, these lost souls, with their limited intelligence, engage in harmful, unbeneficial activities aimed at the destruction of the world.

- **Driven by Insatiable Lust & Pride:** They take shelter of insatiable lust (*kama*), hypocrisy, pride, and arrogance. Illusioned by such a mentality, they are always sworn to unclean work, captivated by the impermanent.

- **Anxiety and Endless Desire:** They believe that sense gratification is the ultimate goal of life, and their anxiety remains immeasurable until death. Bound by a vast network of desires and absorbed in lust and anger, they unscrupulously accumulate wealth for sensual enjoyment.

- **Egotistical Delusions:** They think: "I have gained so much today, and I will fulfill this desire. This much is mine, and more will be mine next year. That enemy I have slain, and others also I shall slay. I am the lord, the enjoyer. I am perfect, powerful, happy & rich. Who is equal to me? I shall perform sacrifices, give charity, and thus I shall rejoice." Deluded by such ignorance, they become entangled.

- **Descent into Lower States:** Bewildered by numerous anxieties, enmeshed in a web of illusions, and overly addicted to sense pleasure, they fall into hellish conditions of existence, life after life. Krishna states that such envious and mischievous individuals, the lowest among men, are repeatedly cast by Him into demoniac wombs.

The Three Gates to Self-Destruction: Krishna emphatically identifies three primary vices that act as gateways to this self-destructive, hellish existence: **Lust (Kama), Anger (Krodha), and Greed (Lobha).** He urges that every sane person must give up these three, as they lead to the degradation of the soul (BG 16.21-22). One who is free from these three gates of darkness practices what is auspicious for oneself and thus gradually attains the supreme destination.

The Authority of Wisdom Teachings: In contrast to those who follow their own whims, Krishna stresses the importance of adhering to the guidance of wisdom teachings (scriptures) to understand what constitutes duty and what should not be done. *"He who discards scriptural injunctions and acts according to his own whims attains neither perfection, nor happiness, nor the supreme destination. Therefore, one should understand what is duty and what is not duty by the regulations of the scriptures. Knowing such rules and regulations, one should act so that he may gradually be elevated."* (BG 16.23-24).

Transformation Strategies: Practical Methods for Transforming Negative Tendencies into Positive Strengths

The delineation of divine and demoniac qualities is not to condemn, but to enlighten and empower us to choose our path consciously. We all possess a mixture of these tendencies. The spiritual journey involves a sustained effort to cultivate the divine and diminish the demoniac within. Here are practical strategies for this inner transformation:

1. **Conscious Awareness and Choice:** The very first step is to honestly recognize these qualities within ourselves through impartial self-observation, without falling into excessive guilt or defensiveness. Acknowledge your patterns, and then make a firm resolve to cultivate the positive.

2. **Cultivating Opposite Virtues (Pratipaksha Bhavana):** This is a powerful yogic technique. When a negative (Asuri) thought or emotion arises (e.g., anger, greed, envy), consciously and deliberately cultivate its opposite divine (Daivi) quality (e.g., forgiveness, contentment, appreciation for others).

3. **Mindfulness and the Sacred Pause:** Practice mindfulness to become aware of thoughts and impulses *before* they translate into harmful speech or action. Create a "sacred pause" between stimulus and response, giving yourself a chance to choose a more divine reaction.

4. **Satsanga (Association with the Virtuous):** The company we keep significantly influences our consciousness. Seek out and spend time with people who embody divine qualities, whose actions and words inspire you towards goodness.

5. **Study and Contemplation of Wisdom (Svadhyaya):** Regularly engage with sacred texts like the Bhagavad Gita and other wisdom traditions. Contemplate their teachings on virtue, ethics, and spiritual growth.

6. **Selfless Service (Karma Yoga):** Engaging in actions for the welfare of others without expecting personal reward naturally diminishes ego, selfishness, and greed.

7. **Devotional Practices (Bhakti Yoga):** Connecting with the Supreme Lord through prayer, chanting, and remembrance purifies the heart and mind, making it easier for divine qualities to blossom. As one draws closer to the Supremely Pure, His qualities are reflected in the devotee.

8. **Small, Consistent Efforts:** Lasting transformation is usually a gradual process, not an overnight miracle. Focus on making small, consistent efforts every day to cultivate one or two divine qualities or to overcome a specific negative tendency. Every conscious choice for the better matters.

Chapter 16 Takeaway: Your Character, Your Destiny – Choose Wisely

Daivasura Sampad Vibhaga Yoga provides us with an invaluable map of our inner landscape, clearly charting the qualities that lead to liberation and those that lead to bondage. We all have the innate capacity for divine virtues, and we all grapple with tendencies that can pull us down. The profound message of this chapter is one of empowerment: our character is not fixed, and our destiny is not sealed. By understanding these contrasting natures, by making a conscious and consistent choice to cultivate divine qualities, by adhering to the wisdom of sacred teachings rather than the dictates of our lower impulses, and by actively transforming our negative habits, we can consciously shape our character and steer our lives towards lasting peace, true happiness, and the realization of our highest spiritual potential. This choice, made daily, is fundamental to our growth and freedom.

दैवी सम्पद्वमिोक्षाय नबिन्धायासुरी मता । मा शुचः सम्पदं दैवीमभजितोऽसपािण्डव ॥ १६.५ ॥

Daivī sampad vimokṣāya nibandhāyāsurī matā | Mā śucaḥ sampadaṁ daivīm abhijāto 'si pāṇḍava || 16.5 ||

Hindi: "दैवी सम्पदा वमिुक्तिके लयि और आसुरी सम्पदा बन्धन के लयि मानी गयी है। हे पाण्डुपुत्र! तुम शोक मत करो, क्योंकि तुम दैवी सम्पदा को प्राप्त हुए हो।"

English: "The transcendental qualities are conducive to liberation, whereas the demoniac qualities make for bondage. Do not worry, O son of Pāṇḍu, for you are born with the divine qualities." ***(This verse clearly distinguishes the outcome of divine versus demoniac natures and reassures Arjuna.)***

Exercise: Practices for Cultivating Ethical Conduct and Spiritual Virtues

These exercises are designed to help you identify and consciously cultivate divine qualities while transforming negative tendencies.

1. **Practice: Virtue Embodiment for the Week:**

Choose a Divine Quality: From the list of Daivi Sampad (e.g., fearlessness, nonviolence, truthfulness, freedom from anger, compassion, forgiveness, tranquility), select one quality that you particularly wish to develop or strengthen in yourself this week.

Daily Focus & Practice:

- Each morning, briefly reflect on the meaning of this virtue and set an intention to embody it throughout your day.
- Actively look for opportunities to practice this quality in your thoughts, words, and actions – in your interactions at home, at work (e.g., dealing with colleagues in Mumbai's competitive environment), and in your community.
- At the end of each day, journal briefly: How did you practice this virtue? What challenges did you face? What did you learn?

Weekly Review: At the end of the week, review your experiences. How has focusing on this virtue impacted your inner state and your interactions?

2. **Practice: Transforming a Negative Habit Loop with its Divine Opposite:**

Identify a Negative Tendency: Choose one specific negative tendency or habit (rooted in Asuri Sampad, e.g., a tendency towards harsh speech when stressed, procrastination due to inertia, feeling envious of others' success) that you would like to transform.

Analyze the Loop: What are the typical triggers for this tendency? What are your usual thoughts, feelings, and actions when it arises? What are the immediate (often temporary) "payoffs" and the long-term negative consequences?

Identify the Divine Opposite: What divine quality (from the Daivi Sampad list) is the direct antidote or positive counterpart to this negative tendency? (e.g., Opposite of harsh speech is gentle/truthful speech; opposite of procrastination is proactive effort/vigor; opposite of envy is appreciating others/contentment).

Create an "If-Then" Transformation Plan: Formulate a simple plan: "If [my specific trigger for the negative habit] occurs, then I will consciously pause, take a breath, and choose to practice [the opposite divine quality/action]." Visualize yourself successfully doing this.

Practice & Observe: Implement this plan consistently. Be patient with yourself; change takes effort. Observe any shifts, however small.

3. **Reflection Practice: Identifying Your Inner 'Devas' and 'Asuras':**

Honest Self-Assessment: Take some quiet time to honestly reflect on the lists of divine and demoniac qualities provided in this chapter.

Strengths to Nurture: Which two or three divine qualities (Deva traits) do you feel are already somewhat developed or naturally present in you? How can you nurture and strengthen them further?

Challenges to Address: Which two or three demoniac tendencies (Asura traits) do you recognize as personal challenges that you sometimes struggle with or need to consciously work on transforming?

Journal your reflections without harsh judgment, but with a clear intention for growth.

4. **Reflection Practice: Navigating the 'Three Gates' (Lust, Anger, Greed):**

Lord Krishna identifies lust (excessive desire, *kama*), anger (*krodha*), and greed (*lobha*) as three destructive gates that lead to self-degradation.

Personal Observation: In what ways, subtle or overt, have you observed these three tendencies manifesting in your own life or in the world around you (e.g., in societal pressures, media, workplace dynamics)? How do they impact peace and well-being?

Strategies for Mitigation: Based on the Gita's teachings so far (Karma Yoga, Dhyana Yoga, Jnana Yoga, Bhakti Yoga, and the cultivation of divine qualities), what practical steps can you begin to take to reduce the power and influence of lust, anger, and greed in your life? Journal your ideas.

(Choosing your higher path is an ongoing, moment-to-moment practice. By consciously cultivating divine virtues and understanding the pitfalls of demoniac tendencies, you empower yourself to live a life aligned with your true spiritual nature, leading to greater peace, purpose, and freedom.)

Adhyay 17: Faith That Sets You Free – Building Beliefs That Empower You

(Sraddhatraya Vibhaga Yoga – The Yoga of the Division of the Three Kinds of Faith)

Beyond the Letter: The Spirit of True Worship

In Adhyay 16, Lord Krishna starkly contrasted the divine and demoniac natures, emphasizing that those who disregard scriptural injunctions and act whimsically according to their lower impulses head towards bondage. This naturally leads to a practical question, which Arjuna poses at the beginning of this chapter: What is the spiritual standing of those who may not meticulously follow all the detailed rules and regulations of the scriptures, yet who perform worship and other duties with sincere faith (*Sraddha*) according to their own inherent nature? Are their efforts Sattvic, Rajasic, or Tamasic?

This inquiry is vital for anyone navigating their spiritual path in the modern world, where strict adherence to ancient scriptural rituals might not always be feasible or fully understood. Krishna's response forms the essence of *Sraddhatraya Vibhaga Yoga* – the yoga of understanding the three divisions of faith. He reveals that faith itself, like all aspects of our material existence, is colored by the three Gunas (Sattva, Rajas, and Tamas). Understanding this classification empowers us to consciously cultivate a faith that is pure, uplifting, and truly liberating, a faith that builds an empowering belief system.

The Power of Belief: How Different Types of Faith Shape Your Actions and Reality

Lord Krishna begins by affirming the fundamental role of faith: *"O son of Bharata, the faith of embodied beings is of three kinds, according to their acquired nature (influenced by the Gunas). Hear now about this. The living being is said to be of a particular faith according to the modes he has acquired."* (BG 17.2-3, paraphrased). In essence, **you are what your faith is.**

Sraddha is more than just intellectual assent or blind belief. It is a deep-seated conviction, a potent trust, an earnestness that shapes our entire worldview, our values, our goals, and consequently, our actions and experiences. Everyone possesses faith; the crucial difference lies in the *quality* of that faith and where it is placed.

- Our core beliefs – about ourselves, about the world, about what is ultimately real and valuable, about the nature of the Divine – act like a lens through which we perceive reality.
- This lens of faith determines what we strive for, what sacrifices we are willing to make, how we interpret life's challenges and successes, and ultimately, the kind of destiny we create for ourselves.
- The good news is that faith is not static. While influenced by past conditioning and the dominant Gunas, it can be consciously purified, elevated, and aligned with higher truths through self-awareness and deliberate spiritual practice.

Understanding the nature of our own faith is therefore paramount if we wish to build beliefs that genuinely empower us and lead to lasting freedom.

Three Kinds of Faith: Understanding the Influence of Sattvic (Clear), Rajasic (Driven), and Tamasic (Deluded) Faith

Krishna explains that the faith (*Sraddha*) of human beings, born of their inherent nature, is of three kinds, corresponding to the three Gunas:

Sattvic Faith (Faith in Goodness/Clarity):

- **Nature:** This faith is pure, clear, luminous, and aligned with the wisdom of the scriptures and higher spiritual principles. It arises from the predominance of Sattva Guna.
- **Manifestation:** People with Sattvic faith naturally gravitate towards worshipping the Devas (divine beings who represent cosmic principles and virtues, or the Supreme Lord in His benevolent aspects). Their actions are aimed at purification, acquiring knowledge, and performing duties selflessly for the welfare of all. Their worship is typically performed according to scriptural injunctions, without ostentation, and with a desire for spiritual upliftment. This faith leads to peace, happiness, and eventual liberation.

Rajasic Faith (Faith in Passion/Activity):

- **Nature:** This faith is driven by passion, ambition, and a strong desire for personal gain, power, fame, or material results. It arises from the predominance of Rajas Guna.
- **Manifestation:** People with Rajasic faith tend to worship Yakshas and Rakshasas (powerful, often materialistic or aggressive demigods or spirits), or they engage in worship primarily for ostentation, to gain respect, or to achieve specific worldly rewards. Their actions are often characterized by intense effort, competitiveness, and a focus on external achievements. This faith leads to temporary gains, but also to anxiety, agitation, and further entanglement in the cycle of desire and action.

Tamasic Faith (Faith in Ignorance/Darkness):

- **Nature:** This faith is born of ignorance, delusion, superstition, and often runs contrary to established scriptural wisdom or ethical principles. It arises from the predominance of Tamas Guna.
- **Manifestation:** People with Tamasic faith often worship ghosts, spirits, or lower demigods, sometimes engaging in practices that involve unnecessary self-torture, harm to others, or are performed without proper understanding, faith, or respect for higher principles. Their actions are often characterized by laziness, confusion, or adherence to baseless beliefs. This faith leads to further darkness, delusion, and degradation.

Krishna then elaborates on how these three types of faith influence crucial aspects of life: the **food** one prefers, the nature of **sacrifices** (*Yajna*) one performs, the type of **austerity** (*Tapa*) one undertakes, and the manner of **charity** (*Danam*) one gives:

- **Food (Ahara - BG 17.8-10):**
    - *Sattvic foods* promote life, vitality, strength, health, happiness, and satisfaction. They are juicy, smooth, substantial, and agreeable to the palate (e.g., fresh fruits, vegetables, grains, dairy, nuts).
    - *Rajasic foods* are excessively bitter, sour, salty, pungent, dry, and burning. They cause distress, misery, and disease (e.g., chilies, strong spices, coffee, overly processed or stimulating foods).
    - *Tamasic foods* are stale, tasteless, putrid, decomposed, leftover, and impure (e.g., overcooked or spoiled food, meat, alcohol, and other intoxicants).
- **Sacrifice (Yajna - BG 17.11-13):**
    - *Sattvic sacrifice* is performed according to scriptural direction, as a matter of duty, without desire for any personal reward.

- *Rajasic sacrifice* is performed for the sake of some material benefit or for ostentation and pride.

- *Tamasic sacrifice* is performed without regard for scriptural injunctions, with no proper chanting of mantras, no distribution of charity (to priests or the needy), and without faith.

- **Austerity (Tapas - BG 17.14-19):** Krishna describes three types of austerity – of the body, speech, and mind – and then classifies each according to the Gunas.

    - *Sattvic austerity* (of body, speech, and mind) is practiced with transcendental faith by men not expecting material benefits but engaged only for the sake of the Supreme. Examples include worship of the Divine and elders, cleanliness, simplicity, celibacy, nonviolence (body); truthful, pleasing, beneficial speech that doesn't agitate others, and regular recitation of scriptures (speech); serenity, gentleness, gravity, self-control, and purification of one's existence (mind).

    - *Rajasic austerity* is performed ostentatiously to gain respect, honor, and worship. It is unstable and temporary in its results.

    - *Tamasic austerity* is performed with foolish obstinacy, by means of self-torture, or for the purpose of destroying or harming others.

- **Charity (Danam - BG 17.20-22):**
    - *Sattvic charity* is given as a matter of duty, without expectation of return, at the proper time and place, and to a worthy person.
    - *Rajasic charity* is given with the expectation of some return, or with a desire for fruitive results, or in a grudging mood.
    - *Tamasic charity* is given at an improper place and time, to unworthy persons, without respect, or with contempt.

This detailed classification shows how deeply the Gunas permeate our choices and actions, all stemming from the nature of our underlying faith.

Strengthening Your Foundation: Tools for Assessing and Reinforcing Your Personal Belief System Positively

Understanding this framework empowers us to consciously assess and refine our own faith and beliefs, steering them towards Sattva.

1. **Honest Self-Assessment:** The first step is to courageously and honestly reflect on our own predominant tendencies. What kind of food are we naturally drawn to? What motivates our acts of giving or our efforts at self-discipline? What is the nature of our beliefs about the Divine or the purpose of life? Recognizing the influence of Rajas or Tamas is not cause for shame, but an opportunity for growth.

2. **Conscious Cultivation of Sattvic Choices:** As discussed in Adhyay 14, we can actively choose to increase Sattva in our lives through Sattvic diet, environment, activities, and company. This creates an inner atmosphere where Sattvic faith can naturally flourish.

3. **Aligning with Scriptural Wisdom & Ethical Principles:** Sattvic faith is aligned with true knowledge. Engaging with wisdom teachings (like the Gita) and striving to live by universal ethical principles helps purify our understanding and strengthen Sattvic convictions.

4. **The Significance of "Om Tat Sat" (BG 17.23-28):** To further sanctify all actions and align them with the highest truth, Krishna introduces the sacred significance of the syllables **"Om Tat Sat."** These three words have been used from the beginning of creation by Brahmins (those in pursuit of spiritual knowledge) to indicate the Supreme Absolute Truth (Brahman) while performing sacrifices, giving charity, and undertaking austerities.

    - **Om (ॐ):** Represents the impersonal aspect of the Absolute, the sound vibration of Brahman. Chanting Om at the beginning of spiritual activities invokes auspiciousness and connects the action to the Supreme.

- **Tat (तत् - "That"):** Signifies that all actions are ultimately performed for "That" Supreme Reality, without selfish desire for personal gain, with the aim of liberation from material entanglement.

- **Sat (सत् - "Eternal"):** Indicates Absolute Truth, goodness, and all auspicious actions. It also implies steadfastness in sacrifice, austerity, and charity, and any action performed for the satisfaction of the Supreme is also called Sat.

Krishna concludes by stating that any sacrifice, charity, or austerity performed **without faith** in the Supreme (i.e., without being connected to Om Tat Sat, or performed with a Tamasic or purely selfish Rajasic mentality) is considered **Asat** ("unreal," "impermanent," "useless"). Such actions yield no good results either in this life or the next. This powerfully underscores that genuine Sattvic faith, directed towards the Supreme, is what imbues our actions with true spiritual value and transformative power.

Chapter 17 Takeaway: The Quality of Your Faith Defines Your Reality

Our journey through life, our choices, our experiences, and our ultimate spiritual destination are profoundly shaped by the quality of our faith (*Sraddha*). Sraddhatraya Vibhaga Yoga reveals that this faith, influenced by the three Gunas, manifests in every aspect of our being – from the food we eat to the worship we perform and the charity we give. By understanding the characteristics of Sattvic, Rajasic, and Tamasic expressions of faith, we gain the crucial ability to discern our own tendencies and consciously strive to cultivate Sattvic faith. This means aligning our beliefs and actions with purity, wisdom, selflessness, and a connection to the Supreme Absolute Truth, often symbolized by "Om Tat Sat." Such a faith not only brings peace and purpose to this life but also sets us firmly on the path to ultimate liberation and freedom.

सत्त्वानुरूपा सर्वस्य श्रद्धा भवति भारत। श्रद्धामयोऽयं पुरुषो यो यच्छ्रद्धः स एव सः॥ १७.३ ॥ (Excerpt from BG 17.3)

Sattvānurūpā sarvasya śraddhā bhavati bhārata | Śraddhā-mayo 'yaṁ puruṣo yo yach-chraddhaḥ sa eva saḥ || 17.3 ||

Hindi: "हे भारत! सभी की श्रद्धा उनके अन्तःकरण के अनुरूप होती है। यह पुरुष श्रद्धामय है, इसलिये जो जैसी श्रद्धावाला है, वह स्वयं वही है।"

English: "O son of Bharata, according to the modes of nature acquired by the embodied soul, one's faith can be of three kinds. Indeed, a man consists of his particular

faith; he is verily what his faith is." ***(This verse establishes the core principle of our being constituted by our faith.)***

Exercise: Practical Methods for Nurturing Empowering Beliefs and Constructive Faith
These exercises are designed to help you assess the nature of your current faith and consciously cultivate beliefs that are empowering and aligned with Sattva.

1. **Practice: Faith & Lifestyle Audit (A Guna-Based Reflection):**

Choose an Area: Select one of the areas Krishna discusses where faith manifests: Food preferences, the way you engage in "sacrifice" (selfless efforts or rituals), your approach to "austerity" (self-discipline, difficult tasks), or your manner of "charity" (giving time, energy, or resources).

Honest Assessment: Reflect on your typical habits, motivations, and feelings in this chosen area.

- *Food example:* Am I drawn to fresh, wholesome foods (Sattvic), overly spicy/stimulating foods (Rajasic), or stale/heavy/processed foods (Tamasic)? Why?
- *Charity example:* When I give, is it out of a sense of duty without expectation (Sattvic), for recognition or future benefit (Rajasic), or grudgingly/to unworthy recipients (Tamasic)?

Journal: Note down your observations. What Guna(s) seem most dominant in this area of your life? What does this tell you about the underlying nature of your faith or beliefs related to this area?

2. **Practice: The 'Om Tat Sat' Intention Setting:**

Choose an Action: Select one significant action, sacrifice (selfless effort), or act of charity you plan to undertake this week.

Set a Sattvic Intention: Before beginning, consciously connect this action with the spirit of "Om Tat Sat":

- **Om:** Mentally offer a brief prayer or acknowledge the Supreme Source.
- **Tat:** Affirm your intention to perform this action selflessly, without attachment to personal gain, for a higher purpose or for the welfare of others, aiming for purification or liberation.
- **Sat:** Commit to performing the action with sincerity, goodness, and steadfastness, aligning it with truth and ethical principles.

Perform & Reflect: Perform the action with this conscious intention. Afterwards, reflect: How did this intentional alignment change your experience of the action? Did it feel more meaningful or purposeful?

3. **Reflection Practice: Identifying and Shifting Limiting Beliefs:**

Identify a Core Belief: Think about a core belief you hold about yourself (e.g., "I'm not capable of X," "I always need

Y to be happy," "Life is inherently unfair") or about the world/spirituality.

Guna Analysis: Try to discern which Guna (Sattva, Rajas, or Tamas) predominantly influences this belief. Is it clear, empowering, and aligned with wisdom (Sattvic)? Is it driven by desire, fear, or agitation (Rajasic)? Is it based on ignorance, pessimism, or delusion (Tamasic)?

Crafting a Sattvic Alternative: If the belief seems Rajasic or Tamasic, what would a more Sattvic, empowering, and truthful version of this belief look like? For example, if the belief is "I'm not good enough" (Tamasic/Rajasic), a Sattvic alternative might be "I am constantly learning and growing, and my intrinsic worth is unchanging."

Action Step: What is one small action you can take, or a new thought you can practice, to begin cultivating this more Sattvic belief?

4. **Reflection Practice: My Personal Understanding of 'Faith that Frees':**

Based on this chapter, what does "Faith that Sets You Free" mean to you personally?

What kind of faith (in yourself, in others, in a higher power, in certain principles) currently empowers you the most?

What steps can you take to consciously nurture and strengthen this empowering, constructive (Sattvic) faith in your daily life, making it a more consistent foundation for your thoughts, actions, and overall well-being?

(By understanding the interplay of the Gunas with our innate faith, and by consciously choosing to align our lives with Sattvic principles and the spirit of 'Om Tat Sat', we build a foundation of belief that not only empowers us but also purifies our existence and leads us steadily towards spiritual freedom.)

Adhyay 18: Claim Your Freedom Now – Your Ultimate Guide to Living Liberated

(Moksha Sanyasa Yoga – The Yoga of Liberation and Renunciation)

The Final Wisdom: Arjuna's Quest for Ultimate Clarity

We have journeyed with Arjuna through seventeen chapters of profound spiritual wisdom. From his initial despair on the battlefield to understanding his true Self, the nature of action, the path of knowledge, the power of devotion, the vision of the Universal Form, and the influence of material nature's modes – the Bhagavad Gita has unfolded a comprehensive roadmap for purposeful living and spiritual realization. As we arrive at this final Adhyay, Arjuna, ever the sincere seeker, desires ultimate clarity on two crucial concepts that are central to spiritual liberation: *Sanyasa* (renunciation) and *Tyaga* (relinquishment or abandonment).

He asks Lord Krishna to explain the true meaning and distinction between these two terms. Krishna's response forms the essence of *Moksha Sanyasa Yoga*, the yoga of achieving liberation (*Moksha*) through the perfection of renunciation. This chapter serves as a grand summation of the entire Gita, bringing together all the previous teachings and culminating in the most confidential instructions for attaining lasting freedom, peace, and union with the Divine. It is here that we receive the ultimate guide to living a truly liberated life.

True Renunciation (It's Not What You Think): Understanding Sanyasa and Tyaga

Arjuna's question touches upon a common dilemma for spiritual seekers: Does spiritual life require abandoning worldly activities and responsibilities? Krishna provides a nuanced and highly practical answer:

1. **Defining Sanyasa and Tyaga:**

Sanyasa (संन्यास): The sages understand *Sanyasa* as the giving up of activities that are based on material desire (*kamya-karmanam nyasam*). This refers to renouncing actions motivated purely by selfish cravings for personal enjoyment or specific outcomes.

Tyaga (त्याग): The wise declare that *Tyaga* is the renunciation of the fruits (results) of all actions (*sarva-karma-phala-tyagam*). This means performing all necessary actions but without attachment to their success or failure, gain or loss.

2. **The Indispensability of Certain Actions:**

Krishna clarifies that acts of **sacrifice (Yajna), charity (Danam), and austerity (Tapa)** should never be abandoned, for they purify even the great souls. These essential duties must be performed, but He stresses they should be done **without attachment and without any expectation of reward.** This is His final and best opinion on true renunciation (BG 18.5-6).

3. **Tyaga According to the Three Gunas:**

Just like faith and other aspects of life, the act of renunciation (Tyaga) itself can be influenced by the three Gunas:

Tamasic Tyaga (Ignorant Renunciation): Giving up prescribed duties out of illusion, confusion, or fear of trouble (e.g., thinking "spiritual life means doing nothing," or abandoning responsibilities because they seem too hard). This does not lead to the true benefit of renunciation.

Rajasic Tyaga (Passionate Renunciation): Giving up duties because they are troublesome or out of fear of physical discomfort. Such renunciation, driven by aversion or a desire for personal comfort, does not yield the spiritual fruit of true Tyaga.

Sattvic Tyaga (Pure Renunciation): This is the highest form. Krishna defines it thus: *"Performance of prescribed duties as a matter of obligation, O Arjuna, while renouncing all material attachment and all desire for fruit – such renunciation is considered to be in the mode of goodness."* (BG 18.9, paraphrased). One who performs Sattvic Tyaga is intelligent, free from doubt, and neither abhors unpleasant duties nor is attached to pleasant ones.

True renunciation, therefore, is not about ceasing action but about transforming the *inner attitude* towards action – performing it selflessly, as a duty, without being bound by desires for its fruits. This is the essence of Karma Yoga, now perfected through the wisdom of Tyaga.

The Anatomy of Action & the Illusion of Doership (The Five Causes)

To further solidify the understanding of detached action and to help us relinquish the false ego of being the sole "doer," Krishna explains the five factors involved in the accomplishment of any action, according to Sankhya philosophy (BG 18.13-15):

1. **Adhisthanam (The Place of Action):** The physical body, which is the arena for activity.
2. **Karta (The Performer/Agent):** The embodied soul identifying with the ego, who *thinks* of itself as the doer.
3. **Karanam (The Various Senses/Instruments):** The different senses through which action is performed and perception occurs.
4. **Vividhas ca Prithak Cheshta (The Different Kinds of Endeavor):** The various functions and efforts involved.
5. **Daivam (The Supersoul/Divine Providence):** Ultimately, the sanction and support of the Supersoul, the divine will or cosmic forces.

Krishna states that one who, due to impure intelligence, considers only their individual self (the Karta) as the sole actor, without taking into account these five factors, does not see things as they truly are. Conversely, one whose actions are free from the motivation of false ego ("I am the doer") and whose intelligence is not entangled in material attachments is not bound by their actions, even if, in the course of performing their duty, they engage in difficult or seemingly harsh activities (like Arjuna in battle). This understanding dissolves the burden of doership.

Knowledge, Action, and Agent – Influenced by the Gunas

Building on the previous analysis of the Gunas, Krishna further details how knowledge (*Jnanam*), action (*Karma*), and the performer of action (*Karta*) are also categorized according to these three modes (BG 18.19-28). This helps us refine our discernment and strive for Sattvic engagement in all aspects:

Knowledge:

- *Sattvic:* Seeing the one, undivided spiritual reality in all diverse beings.
- *Rajasic:* Seeing different living entities as fundamentally separate due to their different bodies.
- *Tamasic:* Clinging to one type of limited understanding as if it were everything, without grasping the actual truth, leading to narrow-mindedness.

Action:

- *Sattvic:* Regulated, performed without attachment, devoid of love or hatred, and without desire for results.
- *Rajasic:* Performed with great effort, driven by the desire to enjoy its fruits, and guided by false ego and a sense of proprietorship.
- *Tamasic:* Undertaken in illusion, disregarding scriptural injunctions, without concern for future bondage or the violence and distress caused to others.

Agent/Worker (Performer of Action):

- *Sattvic:* Free from attachment and false ego, endowed with determination and enthusiasm, and remaining steady and equal in both success and failure.
- *Rajasic:* Attached to the work and its fruits, desiring to enjoy those fruits, greedy, envious, impure, and easily swayed by joy and sorrow.
- *Tamasic:* Engaged in work against scriptural guidance, materialistic, obstinate, deceitful, expert in insulting others, lazy, always morose, and procrastinating.

This detailed breakdown encourages us to continually assess the quality of our knowledge, the nature of our actions, and the motivations of our inner "doer," striving always towards the Sattvic ideal as a foundation for transcendence.

The Path to Freedom: Achieving Liberation by Releasing Attachments and Embracing Wise Action (Dharma & Devotion)

Krishna then synthesizes how performing one's duties (Svadharma) with the right understanding and attitude leads to perfection:

1. **Worship Through One's Own Duty (Svadharma):**

"By worshiping the Lord – from whom all beings have emanated and by whom all this universe is pervaded – through the performance of his own occupational duty, a man can attain perfection." (BG 18.46). This means that fulfilling our natural responsibilities according to our innate qualities (influenced by the Gunas) and societal role, when done as an offering to the Supreme, becomes a powerful means of spiritual progress. It's better to do your own duty, even if imperfectly, than to try to perfectly imitate another's.

2. **Attaining the Brahman Platform (Brahma-bhuta):**

One who is self-controlled, completely detached from material enjoyment, and has renounced the sense of proprietorship can, through this practice of renunciation (Sattvic Tyaga), attain the highest perfectional stage of freedom from karmic reactions (*naishkarmya-siddhi*). (BG 18.49). Having attained this, one gradually realizes Brahman. The state of being situated in Brahman (*Brahma-bhuta*) is described as being perfectly joyful, never lamenting, never desiring anything, and being equally disposed toward all living entities. In this state of pure spiritual consciousness, one attains pure devotional service (Bhakti) unto the Lord. (BG 18.54).

3. **Understanding the Lord Through Devotion:**

Krishna explicitly states: *"One can understand Me as I am, as the Supreme Personality of Godhead, only by devotional service. And when one is in full consciousness of Me by such devotion, he can enter into the kingdom of God."* (BG 18.55). This highlights Bhakti as the ultimate means to truly know and unite with the Supreme.

4. **Taking Full Refuge:**

Even while engaged in all kinds of activities, one who takes refuge in Krishna, under His divine protection, reaches the eternal and imperishable abode by His grace. (BG 18.56). This emphasizes the power of surrender.

The Most Confidential Knowledge & Krishna's Final Instruction

Having guided Arjuna through the entire spectrum of spiritual knowledge and practice, Krishna now prepares to impart the most confidential part of knowledge (*guhyatamam*), His supreme instruction, because Arjuna is His very dear friend and devotee (BG 18.64). This is the essence, the culmination of all His teachings:

"Always think of Me, become My devotee, worship Me and offer your homage unto Me. Thus you will come to Me without fail. I promise you this because you are My very dear friend." (BG 18.65)

And then follows the *Charama Shloka* – the ultimate verse, the final instruction of the Bhagavad Gita:

"Abandon all varieties of dharma (duties, religious paths, or all other supports) and just surrender exclusively unto Me (Mām ekam śaraṇaṁ vraja). I shall deliver you from all sinful reactions; do not fear (mā śucaḥ)." (BG 18.66)

This is the pinnacle of the Gita's message. It calls for complete, loving, and unreserved surrender to the Supreme Lord. This surrender is not an act of passivity or resignation, but an active, dynamic state of trusting in His supreme will, love, and protection. It means giving up the false ego's desire to be the controller and instead aligning oneself completely with the Divine. Krishna personally assures that He will liberate such a surrendered soul from all past karmic reactions and protect them from all fear. This is the ultimate promise of freedom.

Krishna concludes by advising Arjuna to share this confidential knowledge only with those who are devoted, austere, and non-envious. He emphasizes that one who explains this supreme secret to the devotees performs the highest devotional service and is guaranteed to come back to Him. Finally, He asks Arjuna if his illusion and ignorance have now been dispelled. Arjuna joyfully confirms that his illusion is gone, he has regained his memory (of his true Self) by Krishna's mercy, and he is now firm and free from doubt, ready to act according to Krishna's instructions.

Inspiration in Action: Examples of Transformative Renunciation (True Tyaga/Sanyasa)

The spirit of true renunciation – acting with detachment, offering the fruits to a higher purpose & surrendering the ego – can be seen in many who have lived with profound inner freedom while actively contributing to the world:

- **Modern Philanthropists Dedicated to Service:** Individuals who, having achieved success, dedicate their lives and resources to selfless service for alleviating suffering or uplifting humanity, often without seeking personal fame or further material gain. Their actions are performed for a larger good, embodying a form of Tyaga.

- **Dedicated Scientists or Artists Lost in Their Craft:** Those who pursue knowledge or art with such deep absorption and dedication that personal ego and desire for reward fade into the background. Their work becomes an offering to truth or beauty itself, reflecting a natural state of detached engagement.

- **Spiritual Seekers Living in the World:** Countless individuals who, while fulfilling their worldly duties as parents, professionals, or community members, maintain a strong inner connection with the Divine, offering all their actions, and living with a sense of trust and surrender. They demonstrate that Sanyasa is an inner state, not necessarily an external condition.

These examples show that the principles of Moksha Sanyasa Yoga are not just for ascetics in Himalayan caves but can be practiced by anyone, anywhere, leading to a life of profound meaning, inner peace, and true liberation while actively engaged in the world.

Chapter 18 Takeaway: The Essence of Freedom – Surrender in Love

Moksha Sanyasa Yoga, the final chapter of the Bhagavad Gita, masterfully synthesizes the entire spectrum of spiritual teachings, culminating in the most profound and direct path to liberation: loving surrender to the Supreme Person, Lord Krishna. It redefines true renunciation not as the abandonment of action, but as the abandonment of selfish desire, attachment to results, and the false ego of doership. By understanding the nature of action, the influence of the Gunas, and our eternal connection to the Divine, and by dedicating all our actions in a spirit of devotional service, we can transcend material conditioning. Krishna's ultimate promise – to deliver those who exclusively surrender unto Him from all sins and fears – is the most hopeful and empowering message. This path of engaged action performed with inner detachment and loving surrender is the key to claiming our freedom now, living a life of profound purpose, and attaining eternal union with the Divine.

सर्वधर्मान्परित्यज्य मामेकं शरणं व्रज । अहं त्वां सर्वपापेभ्यो

मोक्षयिष्यामि मा शुचः ॥ १८.६६ ॥

Sarva-dharmān parityajya mām ekaṁ śaraṇaṁ vraja | Ahaṁ

tvāṁ sarva-pāpebhyo mokṣayiṣyāmi mā śucaḥ || 18.66 ||

Hindi: "सम्पूर्ण धर्मों को अर्थात् सम्पूर्ण कर्तव्यकर्मों को मुझमें त्यागकर तू केवल एक मुझ सर्वशक्तिमान्, सर्वाधार परमेश्वर की ही शरण में आ जा। मैं तुझे सम्पूर्ण पापों से मुक्त कर दूँगा, तू शोक मत कर।"

English: "Abandon all varieties of dharma and just surrender exclusively unto Me. I shall deliver you from all sinful reactions; do not fear."

Exercise: Detailed Practices and Reflections for Sustained Inner Peace and Living a Liberated Life

These final exercises are designed to help you integrate the culminating wisdom of the Gita, focusing on true renunciation, surrender, and aligning your life with your highest spiritual purpose.

1. **Practice: Identifying and Practicing Sattvic Tyaga (Renunciation in Goodness):**

Identify a Prescribed Duty: Think of one specific duty or responsibility in your life (professional, familial, social) that you find challenging, or perhaps one you perform mechanically or with some underlying resentment or desire for a specific reward.

Reframe with Sattvic Intention: Consciously decide to perform this duty for a week with the spirit of Sattvic Tyaga:

- As an obligation, simply because it is your right duty to perform.
- Without attachment to the specific outcome or personal praise/blame.

- As an offering to the Supreme or for the greater good.

Observe & Journal: At the end of the week, reflect on your experience. Did this shift in inner attitude change how you felt while performing the duty? Did it reduce stress or increase a sense of inner peace or purpose connected to that action?

2. **Practice: An Act of Conscious Surrender:**

Choose a Concern: Identify one specific worry, fear, or problem in your life that is currently causing you anxiety or that you feel overly controlling about.

The Ritual of Letting Go: Find a quiet moment. Write down this concern on a piece of paper. Then, consciously and prayerfully, offer it to the Divine/Supreme Will. You might say silently or aloud: "I have done what I can. I now surrender this situation and its outcome to You. May Your wisdom and grace guide it. I release my anxious grip."

Optional: You might safely burn the piece of paper (if appropriate) as a symbol of release, or place it in a designated "surrender box."

Observe the Shift: Notice any feeling of lightness, relief, or trust that arises from this conscious act of surrender. Remind yourself of this surrender whenever anxiety about the issue resurfaces.

3. **Reflection Practice: Understanding and Embracing Krishna's Ultimate Instruction (BG 18.66):**

Deep Contemplation: Spend at least 15-20 minutes meditating on or deeply contemplating the meaning of BG 18.66: *"Abandon all varieties of dharma and just surrender exclusively unto Me. I shall deliver you from all sinful reactions; do not fear."*

Personal Meaning:

- What does "abandon all varieties of dharma" mean to you in a practical sense? It doesn't mean abandoning your responsibilities, but perhaps abandoning your ultimate *reliance* on them or your egoistic attachment to performing them perfectly for your own salvation, in favor of ultimate reliance on the Supreme.
- What does "surrender exclusively unto Me" feel like or imply for you? What fears or resistances arise, if any? What would it take to cultivate such deep trust?
- How does the assurance "I shall deliver you... do not fear" impact you?

Journal your deepest reflections, questions, and feelings about this ultimate instruction.

4. **Reflection Practice: Your Personal Path to Liberation – Integrating the Gita's Wisdom:**

Review Your Journey: Think back over the key teachings of the Bhagavad Gita as presented in this book – understanding your true Self, selfless action (Karma Yoga), the path of knowledge (Jnana Yoga), meditation (Dhyana Yoga), devotion (Bhakti Yoga), understanding the Gunas, and true renunciation.

Identify Key Resonances: Which one or two principles or practices from the Gita resonate most deeply with you at this point in your life? Which ones feel most crucial or inspiring for your personal path towards greater peace, purpose, and inner freedom?

Commitment to Integration: What is one concrete commitment you can make to yourself to more consistently integrate these key principles or practices into your daily life moving forward from today? Be specific and realistic.

Write down your key insights and your commitment as a guiding reminder for your ongoing journey.

(Living a liberated life is the culmination of understanding, practice, and grace. The Bhagavad Gita offers the complete path. By embracing its wisdom with a sincere heart and consistent effort you live a life of profound peace, purpose, and joy, eternally connected to the Divine.)

Conclusion: Your Battlefield, Your Victory – Living a Transformed Life

Our journey through the eighteen chapters of the Bhagavad Gita has been an exploration of timeless wisdom, a deep dive into the art of living with purpose, clarity, and unwavering inner peace. We began with Arjuna, a celebrated warrior, paralyzed by despair on the brink of a momentous battle. We walked with him as Lord Krishna, his divine guide and friend, illuminated the path out of confusion, not by offering easy escapes, but by revealing profound truths about our true Self, the nature of reality, the meaning of action, and our eternal connection to the Divine.

The Gita, as we've discovered, is far more than an ancient scripture or a philosophical treatise. It is a practical manual for navigating the complexities of modern life, a compassionate friend in moments of doubt, and a powerful catalyst for inner transformation. Its battlefield, Kurukshetra, is a metaphor for the inner conflicts we all face – the struggles between duty and desire, fear and courage, ignorance and wisdom. And Arjuna's ultimate readiness to act with clarity and conviction is a testament to the transformative power of these sacred teachings.

Bringing It All Together: Making Gita Wisdom Your Lifelong Companion

Throughout this guide, we have explored the multifaceted wisdom of the Gita, a tapestry woven with key threads:

- **Understanding Your True Self (Atman):** Recognizing that you are not merely this temporary body or fleeting mind, but an eternal, indestructible spiritual being, a spark of the Divine. This is the bedrock of fearlessness and inner peace.
- **The Path of Selfless Action (Karma Yoga):** Learning to perform your duties with dedication and skill, without attachment to the results, transforming work into a form of worship & means of purification.
- **The Power of Knowledge (Jnana Yoga):** Cultivating the wisdom to discriminate between the real and the unreal, the eternal and the temporary, thereby dispelling the ignorance that binds us.
- **The Strength of Devotion (Bhakti Yoga):** Nurturing a heartfelt, loving connection with the Supreme Lord, understanding this as a direct and

joyful path to experiencing divine grace and liberation.

- **Mastery of the Mind & Senses (Dhyana Yoga & Understanding the Gunas):** Practicing meditation and self-control to quiet the turbulent mind. Understanding the influence of 3-Gunas (Sattva, Rajas, Tamas) to navigate energies with awareness.
- **The Essence of True Renunciation (Tyaga & Sanyasa):** Realizing that freedom comes not from abandoning action, but from renouncing selfish desire, the ego of doership, and ultimately, by surrendering with love and trust to the Divine Will.

These are not just concepts to be intellectually understood; they are principles to be lived, tools to be wielded on your own inner battlefield. The Bhagavad Gita is not a book to be read once and placed on a shelf. It is a lifelong companion, a source of perennial wisdom to which you can return again and again for guidance, inspiration, and solace. I encourage you to revisit its chapters, reflect on its verses, consistently practice the exercises shared, and allow its teachings to seep deeply into your consciousness. Let its wisdom become the compass that guides your thoughts, words, and actions.

Walking Forward with Courage, Clarity, and Calm Confidence

The challenges of life will continue to arise. Your personal Kurukshetras – whether they manifest as professional hurdles, relationship difficulties, health concerns, or existential questions – are inevitable. But you no longer need to face them with despair or confusion. The Gita has equipped you with a powerful arsenal of inner resources:

- **Courage:** A courage born not from arrogance, but from the deep understanding of your eternal Self, your connection to the all-powerful Divine, and the knowledge that you are merely an instrument for a higher purpose.
- **Clarity:** The ability to see situations with wisdom, to discriminate between what truly matters and what is fleeting, to understand your Svadharma (your unique duties and purpose), and to recognize the play of the Gunas in yourself and the world.
- **Calm Confidence:** An unshakeable inner peace that arises from detachment from outcomes, from the discipline of a controlled mind, and from the profound security found in faith and loving surrender to the Supreme.

Remember, this journey of transformation is about progress, not instant perfection. There will be moments of doubt, times when old habits resurface. Be patient and compassionate with yourself. Every conscious choice to apply these principles, every small step taken towards self-awareness and selfless action, is a victory. Embrace the path with dedication, knowing that the Gita's wisdom is there to support and uplift you.

Your Contribution: Sharing Your Light with the World

As you integrate the teachings of the Bhagavad Gita into your life, a natural transformation occurs. The inner peace, clarity, and purpose you cultivate will inevitably begin to radiate outwards, touching the lives of those around you. A life lived with wisdom and compassion becomes a source of inspiration and strength for others.

The ultimate victory on your inner battlefield is not just a personal triumph; it has a ripple effect. When you live in alignment with your true Self and your unique Svadharma, guided by selfless action and loving devotion, you naturally contribute to the well-being of the world. You become a channel for positivity, understanding, and harmony.

So, walk forward with the courage of Arjuna, the wisdom of Krishna, and the love that connects all beings. Embrace your unique potential, share your authentic light, and make your own invaluable contribution to creating a more conscious, compassionate, and purposeful world.

The teachings of the Gita provide not only the solace of inner peace and clarity but also the empowerment to live a life of authenticity, compassion, and unshakable freedom.

Remember, the journey to liberation is ongoing. Every step you take, brings you closer to understanding your true nature and living in joyful harmony with the Divine. Embrace this path with patience, dedication, and an open heart, knowing that the ultimate reward is a life lived in alignment with your eternal, unchanging Self – a life truly victorious.

GROWTH VIDHYAPEETH

Transforming Lives through Love, Peace, Knowledge & Celebration

Growth Vidhyapeeth is an organisation that empowers every individual on a journey where they find & fulfil their unique purpose in the world, unleash their true potential and achieve Love, Peace, Knowledge & Celebration along the way.

Our diverse workshop designs, consultancy & counselling services caters to one-n-all audiences right from Corporations, Entrepreneurs, Professionals, Students, Kids & Teenagers to Families & the Elderly.

Since its inception in 2003, our organisation has managed to create a significant impact in Personal & Professional lives of more than 3L+ individuals across 87 cities worldwide

OurWorkshops:-

ROAR..............Leadership.........Training

Your First Step Towards Being A Magnetic Leader

A highly personalised, intense & practical training module that mentors people with the right skills, knowledge, and mindset required to excel as Trainers on a Global stage.

Life Vidhyapeeth (LVP)

Connect to Happiness: Recreate-Rejuvenate-Reinvent

A Program is designed to empower you to Explore your true Potential, Find Inner Joy & Create a Life of Purpose and Fulfilment.

Business Vidyapeeth (BVP)

Journey towards Building A Visionary Organization

The ideal mentorship model for Entrepreneurs & Business Owners who aspire to unchain themselves from the usual Business routine towards building a Visionary Organization.

The Missing Piece To Success (TMPS)
7 Best Practices to be amongst the Top 1% Achievers.

The course is meticulously designed to propel you towards breaking limitations, embracing a winner's mindset & achieving remarkable success on all fronts.

Super Memory Master (SM2)
Memory & Study Skills Solution For 5th Std To Graduates

Best scientific techniques that help you Master the process of Faster Remembering, Higher Recall & Better Concentration.

Super Power Projection For Teenagers (SP2T)
Empower-Encourage-Channelize Youth

Workshop that helps teenagers overcome their fears, harness their strengths, explore their true potential and channelise their ENERGY in the right direction

Corporate Vidhyapeeth
Customised Team Training Modules at Executive, Managerial & Leadership Level

Communication | Sales Strategy | Increasing Work Efficiency | Stress Management | Employee Engagement | Integrity | Mindfulness | Leadership

Powerful Kids Vidhyapeeth (PKV)
Beyond Curriculums To All-Round Growth

Follow Us

https://www.facebook.com/growthvidhyapeeth
https://www.instagram.com/growthvidhyapeeth/
https://www.youtube.com/@growthvidhyapeeth

www.ingramcontent.com/pod-product-compliance
Lightning Source LLC
Chambersburg PA
CBHW050013170726
48282CB00025B/389
* 9 7 8 8 1 9 6 5 2 5 6 2 0 *